WRITING FOR WELLBEING

This book is dedicated to the memory of my parents, Sarah and Robert.

Patricia McAdoo

Writing For Wellbeing

CURRACH
PRESS

First edition, 2013, published by
CURRACH PRESS
55A Spruce Avenue, Stillorgan Industrial Park,
Blackrock, Co. Dublin

Illustrations by Eve Anna Farrell
Origination by Currach Press
Printed in Ireland by SPRINT-print Ltd

ISBN 978 1 78218 809 4

Contents

Acknowledgements

I'd like to thank most sincerely all those people who participated in Writing for Wellbeing groups with me and especially to those who agreed to have excerpts from their work published in this book. I am deeply grateful for their generosity. Thanks also to Cancer Care West for permission to reprint items which first appeared in *The Healing Pen*. I'd like to thank Gillie Bolton whose wisdom and judgement has had a profound impact on my work in this field. Thank you to Tim Dunne for helping me find that field in the first place. Thank you to Mia Gallagher, Aine Tierney, Brian Barrington, Paul Soye and Sheelagh Kelly for their advice and suggestions and to Bernice Barrington for encouraging me to write the book and for reading early drafts. A big thank you to the great team at Currach Press who worked on the book. Finally, thank you to Dermot for unfailingly generous support and to Dominic, Leo and Sam for cups of tea at crucial points in proceedings.

Introduction

This book is about a way of enhancing our health that is free and available anywhere, any time. The economic effects of a deep recession have left many of us feeling helpless, afraid and personally stressed. It all seems so overwhelming when everything that is having a personal impact on our day-to-day lives is actually taking place on the big stage of the world economy, far removed from us. Amid the doom and gloom talk, it's good to know about things that you can do to enhance your own sense of wellbeing. This is a book for our times.

Writing can be one such powerful and positive force, something we can always rely on to be there. When all else fails, we can always write! For the price of a pen and a notebook, you can write. I'm not talking here about being the next J. K. Rowling but rather about using writing as a way of dealing with issues in our own lives. And you don't even have to leave home! In her book *Journal to the Self*, Kathleen Adams writes: 'For nearly thirty years I've had the same therapist. I've called on my therapist at 3 a.m., on my wedding day, on a cold and lonely Christmas, on a Bora Bora beach, in the dentist's reception room. I can tell this therapist anything.' Adams writes in cheap spiral-bound notebooks. She calls it the '79 cent therapy'.

I first came across the idea of writing for wellbeing when a psychology colleague lent me a book about how writing can enhance physical and mental health. By then I had an MA in Writing and was busy writing fiction, but writing was something I did in my downtime from day-to-day work. When I read that first book on therapeutic writing, the separate worlds of writing and psychology collided with full force. I discovered that it was all about the *process* of writing not the product. Because I liked to write fiction, writing for me was about endlessly polishing and editing everything I wrote. Writing for wellbeing is *not* about polishing and perfecting writing. It's about *expressing* things through writing about ourselves, our lives. As a clinical psychologist and a writer, you would think I would have known! Alas I didn't and since then I've discovered that this whole topic is something of a hidden treasure.

This book is for anyone with an interest in adding writing into their lives in a way that may enhance their wellbeing. Some people run a mile at the idea of having to write. People often have negative hang ups about writing. Yet once you get going it can be pretty addictive. I was collecting my son from an airport recently and, while I waited, I noticed several people feverishly writing in their notebooks, to the extent that one girl's boyfriend had not only arrived without her noticing but had to stand in front of her for a full minute before she even looked up!

There are those who write and those who don't; and then there are a whole bunch of people in the middle who have never done anything like the kind of writing exercises in this book and might, or might not, like it once they give it a go.

It's likely that you will either love the type of writing that we're going to talk about in these pages or you won't. Here's a clue as to whether you will: if you've ever found yourself doodling down a thought or a poem; if you used to keep a diary as a child or still do; then chances are you will take to this type of writing like a duck to water.

If you're not at all sure, then the answer is to try it. People often come to Writing for Wellbeing groups declaring they haven't a creative bone in their bodies or that they hated writing in school or were 'really awful at English'. These can often be the very people who look up sheepishly at the end of the first exercise and say: 'Give me more.'

This kind of writing is also good for those who write creatively (fiction and poetry) because, while it won't teach you editing skills, it does sort of loosen up the creative juices. In an article in *The Observer* in 2002, Jill Dawson, a Whitbread and Orange Prize shortlisted author, is quoted as saying that keeping a journal has helped her personally 'and also made me a better writer because going over and over something eventually makes it clearer'. The exercises and resources contained here will help any writer and, since I happen to love writing fiction, I can testify to the usefulness of this kind of writing.

These are exciting times for the field of Writing for Wellbeing. In recent years, the two fields of Arts and Health have gradually forged significant links as health practitioners have realised the profound impact that writing, music and the visual arts have on health. Reminiscence and creative writing groups are very popular for older people but therapeutic writing can be used in all sorts of health and educational settings that might surprise you such as primary care, cardiac rehabilitation, outpatient settings for people with rheumatoid arthritis, for people who are on dialysis. Therapeutic storytelling has been used very successfully with groups of children in primary schools. In the field of mental health, recent work in Holland has shown that writing therapy through the internet has proved very successful and is now applied in English-speaking countries as well. Undoubtedly the impressive research results have contributed to its growing popularity.

This book should act as a useful resource to those working in health, social care and education who may wish to work individually or in groups or through the internet using writing as a tool. So for those who work in settings like these, this book may offer some tools with which to begin.

How to Use This Book

There are books you read right through to the end and there are books to dip into and browse through. This book is definitely a 'dip into' sort of book. Beginning with the first exercise and working right through to the last chapter is likely to leave you feeling exhausted and as if you are back in school. Better to roam through the chapters, pick something that sort of jumps out at you and then begin. In this book you will be introduced to the methods of therapeutic writing or, as it is referred to here, Writing for Wellbeing. These terms are used interchangeably throughout the book. You will learn why such writing can be beneficial to your health and how to use the techniques to promote a sense of greater control and wellbeing in your own life. The book provides you with a structure for getting started. Paradoxically, it is structure that sets us free with writing, whether that structure is setting a specific amount of time (I'll write for ten minutes) or pages (I'll write three pages) or indeed other structures such as outlined in the many exercises contained within these pages.

Above all, what I wanted to do in writing this book was to provide an accessible map, a guide to how to write about everything and anything, using tried and tested methods that really work. Exhorting people to write is not enough, even if it is good for you. It's like asking someone to cook without giving them any idea how to do it. Think of this book as a book of writing recipes for you to dip into. Try them out, taste and, above all, enjoy!

The Journey Begins

1

Introduction to Writing for Wellbeing

> I want you to feel what I felt. I want you to know why
> story-truth is truer sometimes than happening-truth.
>
> Tim O Brien, *The Things They Carried*

What is Writing for Wellbeing?

When I was a small child, I spent a lot of time in my grandmother's farmhouse in a rural community in Mayo. In that townland of small farms, no one yet had a television. 'Visiting' was the entertainment of choice. Neighbours called in the evening and sat around the fire, regaling each other with stories, the scarier the better! There was the White Woman in the Ball Alley who terrified passers-by at night, the Headless Motorbike Rider who sped through the fields, the Devil who appeared in a local dance hall to a bunch of young people and, of course, the banshee, which could be heard at times of impending death. These stories were not told as some sort of village folk lore, something that had happened to another generation in the distant past but rather as lived experiences, eyewitness reports, freely embellished with new details according to the idiosyncrasies of the storyteller. I listened, terrified and wholly absorbed.

We are all storytellers. Constructing stories is a natural human process that helps us to understand our experience. We tell ourselves and others stories that make sense of what happens in our lives, stories about the sad and happy events, the people we know, the mistakes we have made, the lessons we have learned, our hopes for the future.

Our ancient oral storytelling tradition has been extended by our ability to write which goes right back to the cave drawings. In their book, *The Writing Cure*, psychology professors Lepore and Smyth outline the origins of writing: 'Primitive cuneiform signs impressed on clay tablets by Sumerians 5,000 years ago were the precursors to one of humankind's most potent tools for expressing meaning: the written word.' Writing is quite different from talking. It helps us work things out. It gives us pathways to memories, feelings and thoughts – often ones we might have entirely forgotten. On a sheet of paper, we can record memories, figure out puzzling events, mourn those we loved, make decisions. And writing is private and always accessible. You can scribble anywhere, anytime. If you have the price of a notebook and pen, you've got the tools of the trade right there in front of you. When there's no one else to talk to, if you can't explain how you feel to anyone else, if you don't even know how you feel yourself, you can always write. In such writing, the truth of how you feel can emerge. As Tim O Brien says in the quotation at the beginning of this chapter, taken from his book of short stories set in the Vietnam War: sometimes story-truth is truer than happening-truth because it makes sense of the experience; clarifies it. Another novelist writing about war, Joseph Heller, began his great novel, *Catch-22*, about the Second World War, in 1953, ten years after the events depicted in the book. Sometimes time and distance allow a clear, sharp focus from which story-truth emerges and makes sense of happening-truth.

Therapeutic writing or Writing for Wellbeing is about making sense of our lives. In the words of psychologist, Bruno Bettleheim, in the opening sentence of his book, *The Uses of Enchantment*: 'If we hope to live not just from moment to moment, but in true consciousness of our existence, then our greatest need and most difficult achievement is to find meaning in our lives.' Our behaviour on its own often makes no sense: why we walked away from a great career, why we left home suddenly. Behind the behaviour is the context of our story. Only then does it make sense. What happens when we write in this way is that we are given an opportunity to examine our own story, all the disparate parts of it, using the tools of imagery and metaphor. These tools allow us to take a fresh look at our birth, our childhood, our present life and examine it, as if for the first time.

Writing for Wellbeing is exciting and wildly different from other types of writing. We can explore our lives in a totally new way, ask strange questions like: if I was an animal, what kind of animal would I be today? Asking this question seems a far cry from just jotting down a few lines on how you're feeling today but it probably gives you a much clearer picture of how you actually are (I'm a grumpy old bear with a sore paw, today or a sleepy lion lazing in the shade). Or we might travel to a mountain top on an imaginary journey and have a conversation with a wizard. The animal and the wizard are parts of ourselves that we come to know and explore through our writing. They cast our knowledge of ourselves in a new light. They help us to make sense of ourselves.

In the closing stages of the *Life of Pi*, the main protagonist has just finished telling his fantastic story of surviving on a raft with Colonel Parker, the Bengali tiger. Even though the two people who have listened to his story love it, they are not happy. They do not believe it.

'I know what you want.' says Patel who has told them the story, 'You want a story that won't surprise you. That will confirm what you already know. That won't make you see higher or further or differently. You want a flat story. An immobile story. You want dry, yeastless factuality.'

Our diaries often capture the minutiae of our lives, the things we did, films we saw, books we read. As a child I kept diaries, some of which I still have, including one memorable list of 'things I can cook' which begins with toast! These factual accounts remind us of what we did, where we were on a particular day but don't reflect everything about our lives: our state of mind, how we were feeling, our dreams.

In storytelling, events in our lives can jump off the page, fired by imagination. We can become Bengali tigers ourselves through metaphor, travel through jungles with guided imagery, tell fantastical stories from the words 'once upon a time'.

Writing helps us to reintegrate our experiences. We are able to tell our own story. And making sense of our experience really helps. We organise and remember events in a coherent fashion, while integrating our thoughts and feelings about these events, even if the event was a very traumatic one. Writing gives us a sense of predictability and control over our lives.

Much of the way we live our lives now is compartmentalised in a way that would have made no sense even a hundred years ago. We are constantly bombarded with information about the various roles we play: in work, in relationships, in family life. There are so many ways that we should be, so many things to learn.

Yet our internal story interweaves everything that happens to us, makes real sense of our life as one whole thing and not just a compartmentalised series of things we must be. A growing body of interdisciplinary research looks at the 'narrative study of lives'. It suggests that each of us carries with us a story about our lives that is continually evolving. The story we tell about our own life gives us a sense of self; who we have been, who we are now, who we might yet become.

In the introduction to her memoir, *Paper Houses*, which recounts life in London during the 1970s, Michèle Roberts, who subsequently became Professor of Creative Writing at the prestigious course at the University of Anglia, describes the process of writing nearly thirty years later about that period in her life: 'Writing this memoir joins up all the scattered bits of me, makes them continuous... Out of what often felt at the time like muddle and mess I subsequently make this memoir, this story.'

In reflecting on our own life through writing, things become clear from what might seem like 'muddle and mess'. As the writer Rachel Naomi Remen says in her book, *My Grandfather's Blessings: Stories of Strength, Refuge and Belonging*: 'Finding meaning does not require us to live differently; it requires us to see our lives differently. Many of us already live far more meaningful lives than we know... People who may see themselves as victims may be surprised to realise that they are heroes.'

You as a Writer
So what has been your own experience of writing? We often associate writing with something we 'have' to do, with work, the sort of 'dry yeastless factuality' that is referred to by Yann Martel in the quotation from the *Life*

of Pi. Many people use writing purely to do functional tasks, to get things done: shopping lists, emails at work, course essays. Some of us also have long memories of having our attempts at creative writing criticised at school or college. Even if our efforts were not criticised, we ourselves may have internalised a strong 'critic', that voice in our head which says that what we have written is pure unadulterated rubbish.

Have you ever written something just because you wanted to? When I work with groups, I always begin by asking that question. Usually a good percentage of the group have kept a diary at some point in their lives (or even still do), a few may have dabbled in writing poems and some may have used writing as a way of figuring things out for themselves. So what about you? Have you ever written something just because you felt like it? Not a school essay, not a report for your boss, not the census form! Just something you wanted to write without really knowing why? Maybe it was a short diary entry or a poem or maybe it was a few pages in which you struggled with some issue that was upsetting you at the time. After jotting down your thoughts in your diary, you may have sat back, heaved a sigh of relief and, without really thinking about it too much, realised that in fact you felt a little better about things. Already, you see, you may have discovered the therapeutic potential of writing.

Writing is Good for You

Now, what if I were to tell you that such writing 'just for the sake of it' can be good for your health? That's exactly what social psychologist, James Pennebaker discovered in his research over twenty years ago and has consistently replicated since: a clear link between the use of expressive writing and improved physical and mental wellbeing. Pennebaker, who is Professor of Psychology at the University of Austin, Texas, began to write following a bout of depression triggered by a rift in his relationship. In his book, *Opening Up: The Healing Power of Expressive Writing*, he describes what happened then. After a month of misery, of smoking and drinking too much, he was alone and isolated from friends. He turned to a trusted source of comfort: his typewriter. For a week he spent anything from ten minutes to an hour 'pounding on the keys'.

From initially writing about his marriage, Pennebaker soon began to write about everything else: his childhood, parents, career, even death. Each day after writing, he felt fatigued but freer. By the end of the week, his depression began to lift. 'For the first time in years – perhaps ever – I had a sense of meaning and direction. I fundamentally understood my deep love for my wife and how much I needed her.' He was fascinated with the effect this exercise had had on his own life and went on to conduct studies on the link between writing and health.

Pennebaker began his studies in the 1980s when he asked students to write about traumatic, stressful or emotional events for twenty minutes over three consecutive days. His results found improvements in both physical and psychological health. People were happier and healthier when they wrote; effects included reduced visits to doctors, positive effects on blood pressure, improved liver and immune system functioning and less use of pain medication. Writing also had beneficial effects on emotional health and enhanced social relationships.

One of the more surprising findings is that many people in Pennebaker's studies didn't write about topics that he had assumed they would see as crucial. Even when people were undergoing treatment for serious illnesses, they didn't tend to focus on their illness or diagnosis. Instead, they wrote about relationships, money, early experiences or other issues that were important to them. Senior professionals who had become unemployed got jobs more quickly after writing but more than half of them did not write about the layoff but instead about marriage problems, issues with children, money and health.

Traumatic experiences such as a serious diagnosis or unemployment often focus people on other issues in their lives like their relationships. It's like a stop signal switches on and people choose this time, when given an opportunity to write, to re-evaluate their life. In the wonderful short story collection *Bull Fighting*, Roddy Doyle writes in the voices of middle-aged men in Dublin during the current recession. In one story, an unemployed man knows he is not going to get another job but that is not what occupies him. He muses instead about himself as a father and is racked with guilt about accidentally running over the dog and then hiding what he did from the rest of the family. When he finally confesses this to his adult son, his son replies, 'We all knew we had a great Da.' The father feels like he will explode with happiness. This is the truth that he was seeking: that he had indeed been the kind of father he wanted to be. And it's exactly the same type of truth-searching that happens in therapeutic writing when people look back on different events or situations and try to make sense of how they got from there to where they are now.

One of the most telling findings of the huge array of subsequent studies by Pennebaker and his team at Austin University is that people write willingly when asked to do so. 'Participants from children to the elderly – from honour students to maximum security prisoners – disclose a remarkable range and depth of human experiences ... Even though a large number of participants report crying or being deeply upset by the experience, the overwhelming majority report that the writing experience was valuable and meaningful in their lives.' (Pennebaker, 1997) People deeply appreciated the opportunity to participate and invariably thanked those running the studies.

Twenty years on from his first studies, Pennebaker reflected on his original research. It was all based on a hunch. It made sense to him that having people explore their deepest thoughts and feelings would spur health changes and his own experiences growing up in a non-self-reflective family with a lot of health problems seemed to confirm this. Subsequent studies by other researchers (and there have been over two hundred studies published to date on the topic of therapeutic writing) have shown that writing can lead to significant improvement in lung function in asthma sufferers, improved immune response in glandular fever, decreased admission rates in cystic fibrosis and improvements in joint stiffness in rheumatoid arthritis. Writing improves student grades, memory and sport performance and reduces absenteeism from work. Expressive writing has also been used very effectively with children, for example, in a violence prevention project in New York schools.

Studies have also found improved psychological wellbeing and a reduction in levels of depression. Research by practitioners from disciplines other than the sciences concur with the results of Pennebaker's work. Gillie

Bolton, working in the UK and one of the foremost writers in this field, has consistently demonstrated the beneficial effects of self-expression through writing.

Our writing over the course of a lifetime inevitably reflects the way in which we change. I've always written during important stages of my life, without knowing why I was doing it. As a teenager, my diary became angst ridden, recording all the maelstrom of feelings that led to such confusion during this time. My teenage diaries helped me to get and then keep a grip on what was happening. Much later, as a trainee clinical psychologist, I wrote in order to understand my own reactions to events. Since then, I've written fiction and poetry. I've written during traumatic times and times of great happiness. I've written to vent rage, to understand, to record dreams, to honour the dead. In 2003 Pennebaker did some interesting work on analysing how writing changes over a lifetime and found, perhaps surprisingly, that people use more future-tense and fewer past-tense verbs as they get older, they use more positive and fewer negative emotion words, and also use fewer self-references.

I hope you get a sense from the chapters that follow of just how exhilarating writing can be. The writer Stephen King wrote a brilliant book called *On Writing* just after a very serious accident which almost cost him his life and put him in a wheelchair for months. Towards the end of the book, he describes his journey back to writing, of how he gradually had to learn the way back as he 'stepped from one word to the next like a very old man finding his way across a stream on a zigzag line of wet stones'. He concludes that writing is about 'getting up, getting well and getting over ... Getting happy ... Writing is magic, as much the water of life as any other creative art. The water is free. So drink. Drink and be filled up.'

In the poem 'Digging' Seamus Heaney describes a memory of his father digging for potatoes. This will not be how Heaney's own life will turn out. Instead, as he concludes in the final lines of that poem:

> Between my finger and my thumb
> the squat pen rests.
> I'll dig with it.

Enjoy the experience, dig deep with your pen but be warned – it may seriously damage your sadness! Gillie Bolton is one of the foremost practitioners and writers in the field of therapeutic writing and has been my mentor for several years now. I don't think I could do better than to end this chapter by giving you Gillie's personal health warning about the 'dangers' of writing!

⚘ Take Care

You are about to enter a danger zone
Wear protective clothing around your heart
Take off your shoes

Writing can seriously damage your sadness
Writing can seriously damage your nightmares
You are in danger of achieving your dreams

Once started you won't be able to stop
Nor will you want to

And others might catch it too
You are in serious danger of learning you're alive
You are in serious danger of laughing out loud
You are in serious danger of loving yourself

If it gets in your eyes, consult your loved ones
If it gets in your mind, cancel your therapist
If it gets in your heart, hold on tight.

Gillie Bolton, *Writing Works*, p. 230 ⚘

2

Why is Writing so Good for You?

How does writing in a simple spiral notebook (or indeed on the back of an envelope) lead to good health outcomes?

While the physical and mental effects of writing have been demonstrated many times, it has proved harder to demonstrate exactly why such writing is good for us, why it improves our health. James Pennebaker, who has led the research in this field, says that 'we're still not entirely sure why it works, but the result crosses boundaries of age, gender and social class'. Below are the current explanations that have been put forward.

Writing Helps People to Develop a Coherent Narrative
If people are given the structure within which to tell a coherent story, it allows them to deal with the emotional fallout of their experiences, both positive and negative, in what is likely to be a more efficient way. Multiple studies have shown that it is the people who develop good stories and are able to change their perspective who are the most likely to show health improvements.

Gaining Insight

Those whose health improved most also tended to use more 'causal' or 'insight' words in their writing; words such as 'because', 'reason', 'understand' and 'realise'. So these writers wrote sentences like:

This happened because I did...

Now I know that the reason I felt like...

I understand now that...

I've come to realise that...

Switching Viewpoint

Pennebaker's research has shown that when people demonstrate the ability to switch perspective they are much more likely to become healthier as a result of writing. For example, if people write about an event from their own point of view and then write about that same event from another person's viewpoint they tend to feel much better after writing. One of the key tools used in therapeutic writing is in fact this business of switching viewpoint and writing in the voice of someone else.

Pennebaker's research seems to show that writing changes the way we think about our own story and helps us bring new and broader perspectives to events. Somehow through writing we get to the heart of the matter through reflection on what it all meant; we are less taken up with the immediacy of the events themselves. It's the changes in thinking patterns that predict health improvements and that is exactly what Tim O Brien refers to in the opening quote of the previous chapter: story-truth is sometimes better than happening-truth.

Life Course Correction

Writing can serve as a way of re-evaluating where we are right now, what events brought us to that point and where we see ourselves going. After twenty years of studying the phenomenon, Pennebaker concluded that the essence of the writing technique was that it forced people to stop what they were doing and briefly reflect on their lives. Remember the quote from Michèle Roberts in the previous chapter about how writing her story thirty years later helped her make a story out of 'the mess and muddle'? That is exactly what Pennebaker is talking about.

Writing Frees Us Up

If we get a chance to deal with things on paper, studies show this opportunity to cognitively process what has happened especially if we are dealing with a traumatic event, actually frees up space in our memory: we function better on memory tests; we remember more efficiently. This may be because we have developed a coherent story, worked things out on paper. In other words, we have cognitively dealt with whatever was troubling us and therefore our thinking works more efficiently and this is reflected in an increase in working memory.

Writing Makes Us More Open

People have been shown to become more sociable as a result of writing. They often tend to talk more openly about the things they have been writing about and also convey how their thinking has changed on the topic.

A series of studies have also tracked the effect of writing on relationships. For example, when people write expressively about recent relationship break-ups, they are somewhat more likely than control participants to reunite with their partners. Similarly, when married couples, recovering from infidelity, write emotionally expressive letters to each other, they experience reductions in depression, anger, and marital distress.

The social effects of writing need not be limited to people recovering from a relationship break-up or to those whose relationship is in distress. In one study of dating couples, one person in each couple either wrote about his or her deepest thoughts and feelings about the relationship or wrote about his or her daily activities. In the days before and after writing, instant messages were collected from the couples. Participants who wrote about their relationship were significantly more likely to still be dating their romantic partners three months later.

But writing can also affect how we interact with other people. Pennebaker cites an example of a woman whose husband had died a year earlier. Before writing she had spent a lot of time with friends who referred to her as strong and courageous. After writing she realised she had felt pressurised into putting on a happy face for this group and she then began to seek out old friends from childhood. Changing her thinking through writing also affected her entire social world.

Writing Has an Effect Long After the Writing Has Finished

In Pennebaker's studies, people reported thinking and dreaming about their writing, of 'being in the experiment' twenty-four hours a day even though they had only been writing for twenty minutes a day. Writing can linger in people's minds for days. In this sense the act of writing can be the beginning of a process that goes on long after we've put our pens down. We may think about what we have written, reread it, write some more or rewrite what is already written. The slow burn factor in this kind of writing can be very helpful in coming to terms with a sense of loss, grief and other kinds of emotional pain or just in helping us to work through to some kind of understanding about an issue that has made us stuck in some way.

And so the research continues. Papers on the value of therapeutic and reflective writing are published on an ongoing basis with promising results. Much of the research is carried out under laboratory based conditions by research psychologists. Meanwhile, the practice of therapeutic writing continues in clinics and hospitals, cancer support centres, schools and many other places. The literature on the use of therapeutic writing tends to divide into the kind of research papers we have just looked at briefly and papers and books written by facilitators of therapeutic writing groups. While the precise mechanisms by which writing has such a positive effect on health outcomes remains elusive, the work continues in research and practice and it is likely that when these two fields merge more closely the exact mechanisms may then be identified.

In the next chapter, we get down to this business of Writing for Wellbeing with a look at the issues involved in getting started.

3

Getting Started

When I was in my early thirties, I sat down to write my very first short story. It was for a competition. The magazine *Cosmopolitan* was looking for submissions and I thought I'd give it a whirl. I remember taking a pen and sheet of A4 paper and starting to write. When I finally put my pen down, I looked at the clock. Three hours had gone by. It seemed unbelievable to me. Three hours! Where had the time gone? I had written in a frenzy of activity, my pen moving quickly under my hand, not stopping to think. It had all been so easy, so effortless.

Of course up to that point, I had spent a lot of time in my life writing. I had written hundreds of assignments for college courses. I had written dozens of clinical reports for work. I had written three major theses but this writing had felt like something completely different. It had felt effortless. I had somehow got lost in it. I wasn't at all conscious of what I was doing. I had never meditated but this felt like what people who mediated described: a sort of being lost in the moment.

Around the same time, I bought a copy of Natalie Goldberg's *Writing Down the Bones* and in it she talked about writing as being like meditation. Natalie knew what she was talking about. She had by then spent six years studying with a Zen master and it was this Zen master who finally said to her, 'Why don't you make writing your practice?' After my own experience writing that story, the idea of writing as practice made sense to me – the idea that you could submerge yourself in writing and come out the other side feeling dazed and delighted.

In this chapter we are going to look at the practice of free writing. But before we get talking about the different methods of therapeutic writing, let's just cover some basics.

Questions People Often Ask

Firstly, there are questions people often ask at the beginning of a group so I'll answer these now because more than likely they are the very same questions you may have.

๛ *Isn't therapeutic writing the same as creative writing?*

Sometimes pieces that people write in a therapeutic writing setting are such that the writer wants to work on that piece and make it 'shine' so that it might be published perhaps. But generally there is no emphasis at all on critiquing or editing or polishing any writing in a therapeutic writing setting. Instead what is emphasised is the use of writing to help express issues in our lives. Therapeutic writing or Writing for Wellbeing is all about the process of writing rather than the product.

๛ *If I do decide to write in this way, how do I know what to write about?*

I've worked with many groups over the years and I have rarely found that people get stuck in the way that often happens in creative writing. You can write about anything at all though there are also specific suggestions that can help and this book contains many ideas, as well as resources with further suggestions about writing in this way. Beginning with a few minutes free writing will usually give you some ideas too.

๛ *I wouldn't consider myself a good writer. I never did well in English class at school. Will I enjoy this type of writing?*

It doesn't matter at all whether you're a good writer or not. Nobody else will ever read any of what you write unless you choose to share it and the more you write, the more confident you will become in your own ability to express yourself. Lots of people have bad experiences in school about writing but it can be really good to change this view of yourself by beginning to write for yourself at your own pace. There is something deeply soothing about the feel of a pen in your hand, letting it travel across the page for a few minutes. It's your own private time.

The Business of Writing: How to Begin

When to Write

So how do you begin this business of writing? Set aside a time, a regular time is better if possible. But one thing to point out at this stage is that this is not something you have to do every day. If you set up an unrealistic expectation that you must write every day, then that way failure lies. You may well end up feeling so guilty about not doing it that you chuck your lovely new notebook in the bin. So have your notebook or diary to hand and write when you can, as often as suits you and your life. By 'a regular time' I mean having a time in the day when you think about writing is probably good – but it is important not to beat yourself up about it if you don't want to write that day.

The American writer, Dorothea Brande, wrote a highly influential book on writing *Becoming a Writer*. The book was first published back in 1934 and is still widely quoted today. She gives a very useful set of directions to this kind of writing:

> The best way to do this is to rise half an hour earlier, or a full hour, earlier than you customarily rise. Just as soon as you can – and without talking, without reading the morning paper, without picking up the book you laid aside the night before – begin to write. Write anything that comes into your head: last night's dream, if you are able to remember it; the activities of the day before; a conversation real or imagined.

Alternatively, you may be a night-time person. The morning just may not be your thing. In *Writing Routes*, Satu Niemenen, describes her night-time routine:

> Morning is a difficult time for me and that's why I have 'night pages'. Every night in my bed I put two pillows behind me, take my glasses and my journal from their secret place. I have a few favourite pens I use. I make myself as comfortable as possible. Then I start ... Sometimes I write few words. On other nights the journal is burning in my hands and seven pages get filled.

What Satu Nieminen describes is how writing at the end of the day can be a sort of emptying out process in which she forgets 'the grief and difficulties of the day, I can leave them in the pages of my journal. So I sleep well.'

You might try either method: morning or evening. Or perhaps you have a long commute by train or bus and you might like to try writing then. In *Writing Routes*, Fiona Hamilton describes the comfort of trains as a place to write: 'Stepping onto a train, you enter a zone removed from life's regular demands and interruptions... The train journey offers an objective correlative for the writing process, the varying rhythms of acceleration and slowing, like the rhythms of language negotiating sense.' It's a case of finding what works for you in terms of when to free write and where. Whichever time and place you choose, what you may well find is that your trusty notebook becomes your friend, your ally in this process.

Where to Write
Don't get too hung up on the perfect conditions for writing (it has to be in my special chair with a perfectly quiet house, drinking piping hot fresh coffee from my special mug). You can and should be able to write anywhere, perhaps even on a crowded train. One of the great things about the popular use of iPads, tablets and laptops is that the generation who have grown up using them, those now in their late teens and early twenties, can hop on a bus and just start working. It's the older folks who may get all precious about the 'when' and 'where' of writing. But interviews with novelists reveal that many of them wrote their first books in the most unlikely of places. Here's Stephen King: 'I wrote my first two published novels, *Carrie* and *Salem's Lot*, in the laundry room of a doublewide trailer, pounding away on my wife's portable Olivetti typewriter and balancing a child's desk on my thighs.' (*On Writing*, p. 178.)

What to Write With
And now to the basics about writing materials. My advice as to what to write with is simple: write with whatever you like but try writing the old fashioned way with pen (or pencil) and paper. People who are used to writing only with computers may be loathe to go back to the old fashioned pen and paper method but I would strongly encourage you to try it. It is different.

Nowadays our communication is so often bite-sized: texts and tweets with 140 characters or less. You might (and probably do) type faster than you write. I would suggest that, in this type of writing, speed is not the essence. If anything the opposite is true: the aim is to become tortoise-like, to slow down, reflect, take time, enjoy and saviour the moment. What you get when you write in this way is a symphony of pen, paper and your hand moving across the page: no background hum of a computer, no tip-tapping of keys, just the barely-there sound of pen or pencil scribbling or the soft turn of a page.

Free Writing: The 'Flow Experience'
Now we come to the basic exercise for all therapeutic writing with which I always begin every group. It's called free writing. Think of it as being akin to the kind of limbering up that runners do before undertaking a long run – the slow stretching out of tired muscles; the warming up. That's what you will be doing too: limbering up before going on to run the bigger distances.

The premise of free writing is just that you write: that simple. Write for a set number of minutes (Gillie Bolton generally recommends between six and ten). Write without lifting your pen from the paper. Write without interruption. Don't pay any attention to your spelling, your grammar, even whether what you write makes any sense at all. The point of free writing is to get a flow of writing going where your pen flies across the page without being interrupted. The biggest danger of interruption, surprisingly, is not from other people but from you, yourself.

We all have strong internal critics in our heads. We don't start out that way. But through our experiences, perhaps with learning to write in school, having to produce written assignments and essays, we develop internal critics who look over our shoulder at everything we write. The internal critic tells us what is good and what is bad about our writing but tends to concentrate on what is bad. Our critic tells us that what we've written is rubbish, makes no sense, sounds stupid.

We are highly sensitised to criticism about writing, especially creative writing. Most of us grow up within an educational system that puts self-expression in writing at a very low place in terms of importance. Therefore, when we are asked to just take out a notebook and write, we may feel that what we write won't make sense. What if someone else reads it?

Free writing gets us over this hump. What is important in this type of writing is the process rather than the product. When I work with groups, I stress that in free writing there is no need to read back through this writing, not if you don't want to. You can bin it, you can burn it but, having said that, reading what you write in this way will reveal patterns, themes.

In many ways, free writing is akin to mindfulness. What happens is what psychologists often refer to as 'flow experience', where you are lost in the process. Central to the flow experience is a feeling of loss of self-consciousness. We are simply lost to the world, immersed in what we are doing so fully that we no longer hear the internal critic carping away in the back ground. We are at one with the pen, the paper and the writing. Later we look up dazed and realise we have written five pages or that twenty minutes have gone by.

At the beginning of every group, we always free write: everyone, including me. There is really only one rule in the exercise and that is to keep on writing until time is called. Natalie Goldberg has written a lot about this writing practice with a strong emphasis on the need to keep the pen flowing, to keep on writing for the time that's been set to the extent that even if the atom bomb were to be dropped in the middle of the writing time, you need to continue writing. Nowadays she includes an addendum to this instruction in her book *Thunder and Lightning*: 'In recent years I've softened. I concede to my writing students, "Well, if you're writing with your best friend when the bomb drops, you might pause to say goodbye. But then you get going again – you don't have much time."'

But what if, in the middle of all this writing, you can't think of anything to write about? What if you get stuck right from the beginning? In my groups I say to people if you can't think of anything to write, then simply write 'I can't think of anything to write' over and over again. Actually repetition can lead to some very interesting writing. Writing the same sentence over and over eventually can loosen up some idea or memory which will tumble onto the page. 'I can't think of anything to write. I can't think of anything at all. My brain is feeling numb. I feel numb. I don't know why but I do...' And so on it continues.

I have done this exercise hundreds of times with lots of different groups and I have never yet found anyone who sat chewing the top of their pen for that time. In fact just the opposite is the case. People often look up at the end of the time, blink and with a rueful smile say, 'I was just getting going! I could have gone on and on!'

A word of caution: this kind of writing, this unconscious flow can access deep, hidden memories. If you think that this is likely, then firstly write for a set number of pages or a set amount of time (say three pages or ten minutes and then leave it). While it is possible to write your way through traumatic or sad memories and, I have seen people do this many times, if you feel that the writing is too traumatic, then stop and go back to it another time or start from a different place or better still stick with the structure of a set amount of time or number of pages, no matter what. Also try to ensure you have some support if you feel you need it: a friend or partner to talk to, someone whom you trust.

Free writing is a great way to keep you writing regularly. It is also very useful as a warm-up activity prior to any of the other exercises in this book. In fact it is best to free write for between five to ten minutes before any of the other work. Why? Firstly, free writing, as has been said, helps to get you in the 'zone' to write more freely. It has a huge effect. It loosens up your writing muscles. It also helps to clear out all the busyness in your head prior to other writing. Gillie Bolton calls it 'the mind dump'.

One of the things that constantly amazes me in the type of structured writing that takes place after the free write is how often what emerges is a meaningful whole piece of writing. This writing is usually in response to a specific exercise such as the ones in the following pages. I've been struck by how often when someone reads back what they have written on a specific exercise how completely wonderful the writing is, how it immediately strikes a chord with other people in the group, how it resonates with emotion, making people laugh or pause to think. Given that no editing at all has taken place, this sense of a complete piece is indeed a wonder to a fiction writer who struggles endlessly to get things polished and perfect.

Try writing when you can, for say five minutes. Don't lift your pen from the page. Set a timer. Just keep writing till the time is up. Pay no attention to the writing itself, whether what you are writing is grammatical or whether your spelling is correct. If you want to and are curious, then read it back or else don't. Bin it right there and then if you want to. Just notice how you feel after this writing practice. Now go on and discover other ideas for writing by exploring the exercises in this book.

Now that you have started to free write where do you go from here? Well, the answer is anywhere you like. The rest of this book is a series of structured exercises but before that we look at the importance of how you approach your own writing especially in terms of not being critical.

4

Moving on to Structured Exercises

Structured exercises mean just that. Instead of exhorting you to write about your life in an open-ended way, these exercises are designed to encourage you to write about one specific aspect of your life. The structured aspect is actually quite important. A narrow focus can actually be a lot easier to follow than a broad stroke exhortation to write about anything you like.

This is a book for people who are not writing in a group although any or all of the exercises here could be used in group settings. To help you on your way, there are some examples of other people writing about the same topic dotted throughout the book. The writing samples here were all written in group settings. They are meant to give you a feel for what this kind of writing is like. They are not meant to make you feel deflated. The people who wrote these pieces had no experience of this kind of writing before they came to a group. I include them only because this is a book, not a group, and most likely you are sitting at home reading it on your own. Reading other people's responses to exercises can give you a sense of what it is like to sit in a group and hear how others responded to the same exercise.

How much time should you spend on the exercises in this book? I have never set times for the structured exercises in the groups I work in. Occasionally people ask how long have they got to write and I usually say as long as it takes but in fact there is a surprising synchronicity to the length of time these exercises usually take. I would still say to you 'as long as it takes' but twenty minutes for any exercise is probably a good ballpark figure. It's enough time to get totally absorbed in what you're writing.

For the fiction writers and the poets, twenty minutes might seem like a walk in the park, as if you're just beginning to flex your muscles. In fact, writing in a wholly absorbed way for that sort of time frame, using a structured format, can feel like quite enough. After all, this is not fiction that you're writing. This is your own life and writing in this way can be challenging. So, yes, the ballpark is in or around twenty minutes – could be shorter or much longer but that's the average.

My advice in tackling these exercises is to begin with a little limber up, a few minutes free writing, probably more than five minutes and less than ten. For free writing, just write in the way described in the previous chapter. Free writing will clear away all the stuff whizzing around your brain. It also warms up your writing hand so you're more in the groove. Now you can come to writing in a more structured way with your writing hand all ready to go and with a clear head. When you've done the stretching and limbering of a few minutes free writing, you might trawl through the book and pick out a theme, then pick one of the exercises and begin to write. Once you've written something, you may want to reread it. This is a very important stage in this type of writing and there's a whole lot to say about it in the next section.

Rereading and Elaborating on Your Writing
You may very well wish never to reread your free writing or even the writing you do in response to any of the exercises in this book again. However, it can be a very interesting thing to do. If you leave it for a while (for example, until you finish a notebook) and then reread as if reading someone else's work, you may find it interesting to see what themes tend to repeat. What is it that concerned you most at this particular time? You may find nuggets of insight into an issue that you had completely forgotten. You may notice how you have grappled with the same issue over and over. You may find some of what you've written interesting and some of it very boring and repetitive. If you do find that the same issue is teased out again and again with apparently no development of insight into it, you may decide to take that issue and try one of the exercises in this book.

In a recent entry on Jessica Kingsley Publishers (JKP) blog on therapeutic writing, Kate Thompson writes the following about completing the feedback loop when rereading your own writing: 'There is one therapeutic journal technique which completes the reflective loop and does much to promote the integration of experience. It is a way of giving yourself a little written feedback after any journal entry.' She recommends that if you are rereading a regular journal that you write a couple of sentences like:

When I read this, I notice...

When I read this, I feel...

She calls this the key to therapeutic writing 'completing the loop' where insights and learning get consolidated.

What happens in keeping a diary, a journal, in writing night-time or morning pages or in writing in response to any of the exercises in this book, is what psychologists call 'mirroring'. When a mother or father holds a baby, we can often see this process. The mother smiles at the baby, makes a cooing sound. The baby blinks and smiles back. The mother smiles some more. The baby gurgles and laughs. The mother laughs too.

It's a wonderful process that every parent knows. Babies don't see themselves as separate people. Mirroring builds a sense of self, a core strong sense of self which is what self-esteem is. I think reflective (which means the same thing as mirroring) writing can do some of the same work especially where we have to work through issues that are difficult to explain to other people. Therapeutic/reflective writing is like embarking on an exploration. We do not know the destination and yet reading back through journals or notebooks can evoke a sense of arrival, of coming back to familiar territory only now seeing this place with new eyes. In the words of T. S. Eliot in his epic poem *The Wasteland*: 'We shall not cease from exploration. And the end of all our exploring will be to arrive where we started and know the place for the first time.'

In our notebook, we can read back what we said or thought. Our life becomes reflected back to us. Things that didn't make sense become clear. Themes emerge. Maybe we write every day for a while about the same thing. It all seems repetitive, muddled, even stupid. Finally, when we read back, something like the same process which happens in mirroring begins to take place. As we read, our inner voice says: 'Oh now I get it. Now I see why I'm always getting so angry about that. Actually I am feeling sad.'

It all begins to make sense: why you kept walking away from decisions, why this relationship ended then, why you never again contacted your friend after that row. Now you know why. You have come a circular route and arrived back at the beginning and you can see the place 'as if for the first time'.

We are so complicated. So many disparate parts of ourselves come into play every day: the interior selves we only come to know through self-reflection: the childish part; the angry part; the resentful part; the sad part; the bereft part; the joyous part. They are all there, some parts more obvious than others at various times in our lives.

Writing can allow us to get to know those parts of ourselves. What is wonderful about this type of writing is that in the safety of our writing we can let these voices speak: the sad or angry or playful voices that reflect this complex interior world. Our notebooks reflect these parts of us.

In reading back what we have written we see these parts there on the page: the angry voice that remembers missing out on that great part in the play; the sad part that is grieving a broken relationship; the part that feels abandoned at the loss of a treasured job; the joyful, happy part that witnessed a wonderful sunset.

You will not be alone when you come to rereading your writing. There will be a very vociferous internal critic perched on your shoulder reading every line with you, tut tutting in places, laughing right out loud in others and muttering all kinds of words like 'rubbish', 'stupid' and a host of others. Natalie Goldberg refers to the critical voices in our heads as 'humming mosquitoes'. This is a very good description of the kind of buzzing that can distract you from reading your own work with what I like to call 'an open heart'. If there is a moment in your life when you should be non-judgemental, then this is it.

You have one big job to do when you're reading back your own work and that is to silence the internal critic. Here you must read your own words with attention and even love. This is what you wrote and this must be honoured for what it is: what Goldberg calls 'naked writing'. Rereading your own work is a kind of self-revelation. You are seeing yourself for what you are. This voice you hear when you read back to yourself is your voice, what the poet Thomas Lux, describes in the poem 'The Voice You Hear When You Read Silently'. He paints a vivid picture of that voice:

> your voice
> caught in the dark cathedral
> of your skull.

Rereading your writing can surprise. In reading back your work, you may get a greater sense of your own life story, of how the narrative of your life holds together, how it all makes sense.

In his book *Culture and Value*, the great philosopher, Wittgenstein describes how writing can do this: 'I really do think with my pen, because my head often knows nothing about what my hand is writing.' The poet, W. H. Auden also wrote about how reading your own words can surprise or inform you: 'Let me see what I wrote so I know what I think.'

In explaining this phenomenon of surprise at what is written the psychotherapist and writing facilitator, Angela Buttimer says: 'Many of us have learned, as adults, to self-contain and compartmentalise our honest and authentic emotions and, when given permission, the process of opening and expressing oneself can be like a flood bursting through a dam when pen hits paper (or fingers hit keyboard).' Gillie Bolton echoes this sentiment in her book, *Write Yourself*: 'Expressive and explorative writing is really a process of deep listening, attending to some of the many aspects of the self, habitually blanketed during waking lives.'

Sometimes when you read your work back, you come across something that seems to hit the nail on the head, a jewel that sort of jumps right off the page. If this happens and, it most probably will, then underline it, put an asterisk beside it. This might be something to write about again, using any one of the ideas from further chapters in this book.

While the process of writing, as it is described throughout this book, takes precedence over the product, there may well come a time when, having reread your own work, you decide either to take an issue that has emerged and try to write about it again or else take a piece of writing and use it as the base to redraft. Fiction writers will take to this process like ducks to water because they do it all the time.

Deepening Your Writing

Once you've started to reread what you have written, you may decide you'd like to write more about some theme that has emerged. Maybe you're just getting through the break-up of a relationship. Maybe you feel all talked out with friends but yet not by any means 'over it' so you may well find that you've been writing a lot on this theme but you still aren't quite 'written out'.

As you continue to write every day or however often you decide to write, you may find that your writing on this theme changes of its own accord. Satu Nieminen describes how in her journal writing she usually begins by writing about what's been happening in her world, then slides into feelings and, after about a month, usually feels that she has come to some conclusion about what theme she's been handling. It may well be different for you but it is useful to be aware of this idea of a rhythm to writing. You may glide across the surface of an issue or tend to dive right in; you might then write feverishly about this issue, maybe writing a lot for the next few days or weeks until the theme somehow loses its power, or you reach some conclusion about it.

Digging deeper (remember the poem by Seamus Heaney in Chapter One) on a theme might mean you try some more of the exercises in this book. Or you might also want to redraft something you've already written.

Rewriting is a different thing to free writing and may happen at any stage once you have done some writing. Perhaps you have read back the pages of your free writing and decided to review and rewrite something. Perhaps you have tackled one of the exercises in this book and now want to polish the piece of writing that you did. Maybe you wrote a poem and while it does express something of what you were trying to write about, you'd like to give it another go. In rewriting you are trying to tackle an issue, to wrestle it to the ground so that it becomes clear what exactly is going on, what this is actually all about.

One aspect of this kind of writing that perhaps needs to be addressed at this early stage is the idea that writing can also allow you to get bogged down. In rereading your writing you may find that you seem to dwell on the same topic endlessly, going 'round the houses' and ending up back in the same place. Sometimes free writing can read back like one long rant about how terrible everything is. I would suggest that if this does happen to you that you 'really need to get out more!' and by 'out' I mean lift yourself out of your current writing and try something different in the way you write.

If you are bogged down then one way forward is to look at the issue you are writing about and decide to use it as material to try a very different exercise. It's especially helpful if you feel that your writing is stuck in an endless repetitive cycle, especially where the cycle is very negative, that you try writing slant. Metaphor can be a great way to explore another side of things, to take an entirely different perspective, to see things slant! Write 'as if' you were a tiger in a jungle or 'as if' you were weather (instead of writing about feeling very depressed and low, write instead about what it's like to be 'in the doldrums', dull weather with low-lying clouds that just hang over you). There are lots of metaphors presented in this book and you can use one for starters. See if it fits (you will know because the writing will flow easily and it will feel right).

You might try changing your viewpoint. Write the same event from the point of view of someone else who was there. Or try writing about it from the point of view of an object like a coffee mug on the table or a picture on the wall, telling the story in a more neutral way than you would, giving a bigger picture.

Or, if you feel bogged down by your writing, then write a letter of complaint to your writing self and have your writing self write back to you explaining things from their point of view. Give your writing muse a name and let your muse write to you or have a dialogue about your writing with it. Ask your muse some questions about it all. Why am I feeling stuck? Why do I write all the time about the same thing? Now sit back and write from the muse's viewpoint. It might surprise you. The muse is part of you too but might give you a different point of view to the 'you' that has been writing so far.

The main point about rewriting is that, unlike free writing which is very flowy, rewriting may seem more like work. As Gwyneth Lewis says in the Foreword to *Writing Routes*, 'Telling your story can save your life but this practice of authenticity requires discipline and many drafts.'

Now you know how to read your own work with an open heart, just the way the mother smiles at her baby with absolute love. This is how you are going to read what you write. Derek Walcott writes beautifully about this process in the poem 'Love After Love', about the process of getting to know 'this stranger who has loved you all your life'. This is the person you get to know through therapeutic writing, this kind stranger who grows more powerful the more you work this way, who loves you unconditionally and who can, in the end, become far stronger than your internal critic. This kind stranger is your internal mentor, the part of you that cheers you on, that thinks you're really great.

Some time ago, a very dear friend of mine died. We had talked on the phone almost every day for twenty years. We had talked all during my years of being at home with babies. We had talked to the background noise of a roomful of children playing. We hardly ever saw each other but we celebrated each other's successes and, if things fell apart, we tried to figure things out. Then she was gone. For a long time I felt frozen with grief. So many times I found myself reaching for the phone to call her because she was the only one who would know what to do. Why? During all those conversations, those hundreds of hours what had we been doing that was so important? I didn't know. All I knew was this overwhelming sense of loss.

Then one day I picked up a notebook someone had given me. It wasn't just any notebook. This was a really beautiful one with ribbons to hold the pages in place. And I began to write. I filled page upon page. The writing began to mirror my life back to me in the way that those long wonderful phone conversations did. It helped me figure things out. When the beautiful notebook was finished and filled I bought another not-so-beautiful one, this time a bright fluorescent pink that was easy to find. The thing is, those notebooks didn't take my friend's place and, of course, I still miss talking to her but they did become another sort of conversation – this time with myself, what Gillie Bolton calls 'a dialogue with the self'.

My dear friend was and is totally irreplaceable. But I do have many notebooks filled in the time since her death. I found a way to read them with attention, with an open heart, sometimes free writing, every so often reading back what had been written and occasionally elaborating on a theme. Did I or do I now write every day? No, not every day. Sometimes twice a day, sometimes every few days. Occasionally a week might go by. I'm not a great believer in the idea that daily journalling is important, though I think when you start this type of writing it can help to set up a rhythm. I have found that, for me, there is an ebb and flow to the process of writing. If I don't get hung up on it, it happens anyway, perhaps not every day but often enough to be a real part of my life. And did the notebooks help? They did. They still do.

Now we move to the second part of the book which is a whole series of exercises, with one common theme for each chapter. In places the theme and exercises are illustrated with examples of writing. It's up to you where you go from here. Any of the exercises can be repeated again and again. The writing will be different each time.

The next chapter takes the theme of nature which might just be a good place to start.

SECTION TWO

Structured Exercises

5

Take a Walk on the Wild Side:
Writing and Nature

Throughout the whole of our lives, wherever we have lived, whatever we were doing, nature was the fundamental stage set, the backdrop against which everything else took place. 'It was snowing the day I left him...' 'The day I finished my exams, it started raining for the rest of that summer...'

In writing groups, the first exercise I almost always introduce is one which Gillie Bolton has used for many years. I call it 'stones and shells'. As a fair-weather sea-swimmer and all seasons dog walker, I spend a lot of time outdoors. Summer and winter I go to the beach at least a few times a week. I also spend time every year on beautiful Sherkin Island off the south-west coast of Ireland. I like to gather shells with different shapes and colours, irregular patterns, unusual shapes and have a bag full from different beaches, some big, some small.

When I work with groups, I place a pile of shells or stones I've gathered in the centre of the table and ask everyone to pick one without thinking too much about it. Then I ask them to write a description of this object using all of their senses: to write about how the stone feels in their hand, to smell the shell, to listen.

Stones too reveal irregular patterns, smooth surfaces, broken lines, all of which can represent patterns in someone's life. The weight of the stone can come to reflect solidity, a feeling of certainty. Seamus Heaney's evocative poem 'Scaffolding' describes the building of a stone wall as a representation of a solid relationship which will remain standing once the scaffolding is taken down.

When someone picks up a shell, they may begin to write about themselves, using the shape and colour, the feel and texture of the shell as a metaphor for their own idea of themselves: a little hole in the shell can represent a feeling of loss, of missing someone. Ridges can come to reflect a certain edginess in personality. People often write about the exterior and interior of the shell, representing their exterior and interior self, what they present to the world, what they hold inside. Memories pour out: that picnic when you were five years old; when you got stung by a jelly fish; your first holiday away with friends and that wonderful day on the beach. Others write about the shell or stone itself, comparing their own life to the curvy lines of the shell. Here is one example.

✤ A Beautiful Shell

I love shells, their curves, their spiked cones at the tips, the opening lined with the pie-crust edging, the curves lined with stripes. A beautiful snail once lived within. In the water, it looked beautiful; in the air, it fell to bits. The nautilus is the most beautiful snail, it swims upside down.

Living inside the shell must be claustrophobic, compressed, not able to breathe inside, afraid of being picked up by a bird or a crab, and eaten. Quite a squash! I would want to get out, to be free, arms thrown akimbo.

We used to collect shells, as children, on the Silver Strand. I remember that soft day on the beach in the morning sun. The tide far out, blue–green water, paddling between the rocks, trousers turned up, looking for shells. The calm water, a warm, still day. Hills in front of me, in a mist, horizon beside them, above the sea, far away. Golden sands under my wriggling toes. Look, a shell, a little crab hidden inside, crab and shell scuttling away. Sun above, a beautiful light on the still, shimmering sea. Rocks beyond them, the clear water above the sand where the shells are found.

Ann Marie Cleere ⚭

Wild flowers are often the flowers which we remember most vividly from our childhood: the hours we spent making daisy chains. Every time I pick a buttercup, I am immediately transported back in time to a hot summer's day on my uncle's farm, to a field full of buttercups. I lay down on the ground and the sunlight on my face was suffused with yellow. To this day, every time I see the vivid bright yellow of buttercups, I am back lying in that field, looking up through this wonderful haze of yellow.

Exercise One: *A Time When...*

One of the easiest exercises of all to begin is to write about A Time When... It's a completely open-ended exercise. Writing about any time when – gathering stones, shells, flowers, berries on your travels – will evoke plenty of memories of A Time When...

Here are two separate memories of two very different landscapes in response to A Time When...

⚭ *A Time When...*

'Will you meet me on Ko Samui for Christmas?'
This was the question posed by my daughter on a very crackly phone somewhere in South East Asia.
'Yes,' was my instant response and then I asked 'where is it?'

I filled a backpack, I was only 52, with the usual supply of unsuitable clothes to meet my daughter on a tiny island off the coast of Thailand. I had the time of my life, lying on a red hammock for a week, listening to the gentle lapping of water at my feet and the perfume of exotic blooms filling my nostrils. Bangkok followed with the noise and chaos of east meets east, east meets west, lounging, smiling Buddhas, shouting water sellers and Indian tailors. Sleeping overnight on a train racing through the night jungle brought us to Chang Mai, craft workers, native dress and smiling children. Pai on a bus with no brakes and a near peep into Burma completed a month of adventure, excitement and most of all a time when I felt young, light and stress free!

Úna McKeever ❧

❧ *A Time When...*

Driving to Indreabhain last Wednesday full of excitement and apprehension, I wondered if I had made a mistake. I was bringing my friend to my 'special place', Inis Meáin. Would she love it? Would she hate it? Would she dismiss it? Or, like me, would she be seduced by the beauty of the place? Since I was a young woman there has always been a time when islands have been important to me. My youthful summers were spent on Oileán Cléire where the light of Fastnet competed with the stars to provide the only night light in that place. There was a sense of coming home for me there and I rebelled at the thought of leaving it each time when college summoned me back to Dublin. I pined for it often in the darker days that followed.

More recently I have walked and loved Boffin, Clare and Turk islands and experienced a similar sense of escape from the business and angst of mainland life. I delighted in leaving burdens on the pier in Cleggan to be collected on my return. And then I found Inis Meáin, the quietest of the Aran islands. Inis Meáin is different. The lacy stone walls divide the hard won fields and shield the potato rows from the wild Atlantic winds. They seem to hold the ancient history of their builders in their nooks and crevices. I was captivated by its ruggedness, it's Burren stone and it's quiet. There are just these walls.

It's a place for being, not doing. There is no hurry, the people smile and tolerate my rusty Irish. The old women are translucent in their 'crios shawl' beauty. The skies are huge, wrapping the 12 Bens, the Maamturks and the Cliffs of Moher in their feather clouds and starry nights.

Inis Meáin has called to me annually when I needed separateness, rest, peace. Would all of this be lost to me by bringing a stranger to its shores? I needn't have worried. She loved it. She walked, wrote, examined the abundant flora and delighted in the *flaithiúlacht* of our hosts. She even got a few *cúpla focail*. Cancer stole my annual visit from me last year. This time it was precious to be back, healthy and well, with gratitude in my heart and my dear friend to celebrate that with me in what is still 'my special place'.

Úna McKeever 🐚

Exercise Two: *Going Outside*

Take a walk. Instead of using that time to think about some issue or problem or lapse into a daydream, walk with full attention to the sights, sounds, smells, the feel of the wind. Is it warm or cold? How does the rain feel on your face? If you live in the city, walk in the parks and watch the rows of daffodils in springtime.

Take your notebook with you or else take the memory of that sight home with you and begin to write. Stop and gaze up through the branches of a tree. Close your eyes and listen to the wind through the branches. Pick up a cone in the autumn and smell it. Be specific in your writing; be vivid in your descriptions with smells, textures, colours. Feel the texture of the wet grass and write about that, the warmth of the wind on your face, the heat of the sun.

Write through your sense memories. Watch how early morning dew sits in droplets on a leaf or a blade of grass. Notice how the blade is bending under the weight. Wake up to nature in all its glory. The smells, sights, sounds and feel of nature are all around us and can awaken all kinds of memories of picnics long ago, a time when you played with someone you haven't seen in years and years.

Writing from nature can give you all sorts of prompts for your writing, not only memories but also to write about the present time. Write about how you experienced the smell of rain on the ground this morning. The sight of clouds skidding across the sky might prompt you to write about a sudden change in your own mood. The great American nature poet, Wendell Berry, wrote 'Better than any argument is to rise at dawn and pick dew-wet red berries in a cup.'

Go on a journey. Sit on a park bench. Take out your notebook and write about what you see, smell, feel, hear; the shrieks of children playing in the playground, the hum of distant traffic, the smell of rain on the tarmac path. Hold a stone, a flower in your hand and start writing with your other hand.

Here is one writer's description of a walk through the suburbs of Galway on his way to Cancer Care West Support Centre.

♋ Costello Road, Galway

Leaving the UGH gate at Costello Road, I am walking steadily toward my destination, seven minutes hence in Seamus Quirke Road. An exciting voyage, an intrepid traveller's challenge, (I thank God not for me) but perhaps challenge enough for some. A trip to remember?

A story to tell, perhaps even a milestone in my life? Could my voyage deliver some unknown treasures, some wondrous and bountiful rewards? Oh yes, my friends and so much more.

You would be justified in enquiring of me as to what marvel of creation can give such promise of fulfilment in seven minutes walking in Galway? How could I possibly merit such priceless gifts for so little effort? Well, my friends, I invite you on my strange little journey along the road.

It is a pleasant walk. Well-loved gardens competing with concrete driveways.

Beautiful roses, hanging baskets, hydrangeas, bus stops, busy people, friendly little dog and the comfort of seeing a green-roofed building ahead for most of the way. I have stepped out this path for six weeks from early August into September: from the hectic events of Galway Races to the certainty of the swallows departure south and the less graceful arrival of the GU students swooping in to fill the gap. I see the summer engaged in a struggle with autumn to cosset and protect her delicate blooms a failing and futile encounter, her strength depleted. There will be no victory here with only the swiftness of submission and defeat in doubt.

I have only now to cross the road. I will be at my destination. It has beckoned me and now welcomes me. What is this green-roofed place? Is it a haven of well-intentioned folk, a cloister of like-minded souls? Can it be a club? Perhaps. If so, certainly exclusive, right of entry screened and limited, welcome only for the fortunate few, the wealthy, the powerful, the influential! My God what hope have I of traversing its hallowed portals?

Well, my friends, the key is yours, you have been chosen by diagnosis, a selection unique to you. You have a lifetime subscription, it is exclusive and has a glorious and exalted list of members past and present. This, my friends, is Cancer Care West.

Cherish the experience, enjoy and savour the friendship, make it yours, wander in or plan your visits, pick your activity, get involved in your courses. All things are here, even temptation lurks under the shelter of the green roof – the beer store and the betting shop! Moderation in all things, my friends. We have arrived.

Iain Mac Clean

Exercise Three: *Trees*

Using trees as a metaphor, ask yourself the unusual question: if I was a tree what kind of tree would I be?
Would I be a big sturdy tree with many branches reaching out or would I be a little young sapling, stretching up towards the light?
Would I have a strong old gnarled trunk or a slender new smooth one?
Would I have visitors, birds, people sitting under my branches or am I a solitary tree?
What kind of roots have I got? Are they deep and long and keeping me literally rooted to the ground or do I get blown about a lot?
Do I shed my leaves, change appearance?
Now write in the 'voice' of the tree itself: 'I am a gnarly old oak tree. It seems like I've been in this place forever. I like it here. It's quiet but I can watch all the activity in the woods. I don't feel lonely really...'

Exercise Four: *Diving In*

A few years ago I was given a photograph of someone diving off the diving board in Blackrock, Salthill in Galway. The picture was taken at sunset showing the clear and beautiful straight lines of a good dive.

What is it you would like to dive into? Maybe you've always dreamed of taking the Orient Express or learning Mandarin or going part-time at work and writing a novel.
What is it that's stopping you?
Now imagine you have done it. You have actually climbed to the top step of the diving board and finally taken the plunge. What was it like? What happened then?

Exercise Five: *Writing from Pictures/Photographs*

Pictures from nature, postcards, photographs can also evoke strong memories. You might take a look at old photographs or you might just imagine (in your mind's eye) a scene of a place you have been, a place you love. Here is one writer's memory evoked by a picture of a lakeland scene.

❧ The 'Dap'

Thursday was his day to go fishing during the summer. May was the important month, 'The Dap'. Already in the preceding months, the Boat, his pride and joy, was stripped of paint, repaired and painted again. He attempted to rope us in. I did it but I cannot remember if I liked it much then! I do know that I now enjoy getting soaked and mucky painting!

The day would arrive, the boat ready, the fishing rods repaired, the picnic packed. Off we would set in the car. Not many words exchanged, Dad was not a talkative man. We would stop in Oughterard to collect the treats and then off to Borrisheen to the boat which had been brought out weeks earlier and put on the shore, the engine tested.

With effort, I would walk down to the shore and try to help to lift the boat and put it on the water. On our way we would have collected the Mayfly, ready to be impaled on the hooks. I always felt guilty about killing them but what could I say as I was about to 'try' and catch and kill a fish. Into the boat and out onto the lake to the right location then set up the rods, taking a wriggling Mayfly and pushing the hook right through its body.

Letting the line drift with the wind, settling the Mayfly on the surface of the water in wait for it to be hopefully swallowed by a fish. 'Hope' being the operative word as I only remember catching one fish in all those fishing expeditions.

The peace and silence was wonderful and it had to be that way because any noise could scare the fish away. I would be bursting to talk with my not-so-chatty father, but no way. The fish were not to be disturbed. Finally lunch would come and I could talk! We would head off to an island and sit on the shore looking out on the lake water as we ate the picnic with coffee from a flask and the all important treat, the club milk. Then out onto the water again for more bum numbing fishing. The thrill when the poor bait was taken and you caught a fish, instructions handed out – 'ease the line'; 'pull on the line' – made me nervous but I eventually pulled it in. My father was proud but also a little envious as I was the only one that caught a fish that day. The only day I ever caught a fish!

Anne Marie Cleere

In the next chapter we look at places and how we remember them, imagine them, relish them and keep them in our hearts.

6

A Sense of Place

We all have places buried within us, rooms in houses now perhaps no longer even there, ghosts from our past, places that exist only in our heads. Dublin City Council commissioned the artist Chris Reid to record the memories of the residents of the old flats around the Liberties area of the city in a series of wall plaques. The flats are seen as part of the heritage of the city and were saved from demolition in the 1990s. Many families had lived for several generations in them. Here are some of the memories recorded on wall plaques around the area:

- I'd be standing in the kitchen cooking my breakfast. I'd pull up the blinds and open the window to let air in. Next thing you see someone gawking in, waving in and taking snaps. Hello, one says. How are you sir? Good. I says. Would you like a rasher sandwich?

- If you really love something and you have it – then no matter what it is, I think you deserve it. We are only caretakers for the things we love. I am lucky to have this flat. It is all I really have and I really adore it. I think I take care of it the best I can.

The poet, Philip Larkin, described this idea of a sense of place that we hold in our hearts very well in his poem about old age, 'The Old Fools'.

> Perhaps being old is having lighted rooms
> Inside your head and people in them, acting.

Places can assume huge importance in our lives. In groups I work with, we write about places we remember from childhood, places of refuge, places we associate with being nourished and replenished. We use exercises using poetry, metaphor and other techniques to provide writing ideas on this theme.

One of the earliest exercises I did when I began working with therapeutic writing groups was an exercise on people and places. The idea for the exercise was given to me by Gillie Bolton and since that time I have used the exercise many times. The idea is simple. The group is presented with two separate sets of cards or pieces of paper. On the first set are the names of everyday places, such as kitchen, garden, barn, bedroom, attic, hidey hole. On the other set of cards are listed the names of all sorts of people we may know: mother, uncle, aunt, father, friend or teacher. Each person in the group is asked to pick a card from each pile without thinking about it too much. Gillie calls the exercise 'In my mother's kitchen'. Having done this exercise many times with groups, I have indeed seen 'lighted rooms with people in them' as a grandfather's garden is recalled or idyllic summer evenings on the beach at a friend's caravan. For all of these people, the places they chose were meaningful and they still carried the memory of them in their heart. This is one such piece in which the writer contemplates the relationship between her husband and the airing cupboard.

Airing Cupboard – Husband

Hot press. Linen cupboard. Linen press. But not airing cupboard in our house. My husband and I disagree about the linen cupboard. It is here that our differences show. Here and the pantry. This linen cupboard was built with storage in mind. It is a long cupboard. Ten feet long and four feet wide. No windows, a wooden floor and joy – five long open slatted wooden shelves on each side. So much space and so much stuff to put in it! It is here I store, collect, keep and can't throw out stuff. At the front of the linen cupboard, near the door all is pretty neat and tidy, but as you drift towards the unseen back, it is a different story. Here are all the things I need ... someday. Here are the things my patient spouse wants to get a skip for. In fact that would be his idea of a wonderfully fulfilling Saturday. Filling a skip with all the things he thinks we don't need ... starting with the Linen Cupboard.

On the multitude of shelves there lie, as I said, the things that may come in handy. Old duvets for the boys when they have friends to sleepover. Old pillows, for those same friends. For party guests when the house gets full to overflowing. Like at Christmas. I counted fifteen extra bodies one night.

'And don't you need extra pillows and duvets then?' I smugly dig at himself.

There are a few suspicious black plastic bags even to me. I really don't know what is in them! But I am sure they are valuable! On another shelf there are blankets – for when we will need them. There are also cot duvets, handmade. Baby keepsakes for our children, I like to know that's where they are.

As you progress upwards, things get a bit more interesting. This is where himself starts to sweat ... There are old and, I am sure, broken computers, laptops, innards missing, dress up clothes. An old grey and red Meccano robot Conor made which had a short life. There are boxes of stuff, important stuff, I am sure. There are old pictures, paintings, old coats, jumpers, jackets. Many navy and red sleeping bags are stuffed in here. Surely they can't all be ours? They lie rolled, waiting for the summer. Oh yes and on the top shelf is where himself keeps the toilet rolls, all twenty of them! He loves to buy things in bulk. Here also he keeps the spare light bulbs and other useful items.

On the ground, if you drop down there under the bottom shelf are a myriad of important things. Hot water bottles, rugby boots and some unidentifiables. My greatest fear is that one day he will just throw the lot out. And not even ask me! A job I suspect he is carrying out under the cover of darkness, starting with the garage. He is happiest when, trailer empty, he is returning from the dump before I am even up.

'What went?' I gasp, leaning out the bedroom window to see a very cheerful himself unhitching the trailer. Suspiciously empty.

'You'll never know' is the answer, 'I will wait for you to look for it', his turn to be smug as I splutter, lost for words.

So it is here we coexist. The gatherer and the hunter in an uneasy truce. On edge. Defensive. Yet at the bottom of it all I don't really care and maybe it would be refreshing to let go. To let go of all that stuff I don't really need or use right now. Though himself's rule for throwing out or recycling anything he has not worn in six months I simply cannot and will not do! However as spring is here, maybe I could tempt myself to a wee bit of spring cleaning, starting with the Linen Cupboard and see where that lands me.

At the very least it will make himself happy.

Triona Byrne

Exercise One: *A Place That Soothes*

Every week or so, a friend and myself, usually after several false starts, finally manage to nail down an hour or so for what we call 'the bog walk'. It's a bog road in the hills above Spiddal in County Galway. It probably has a place name but we just call it the bog walk. Walking there for an hour provides just enough time to catch up with each other. We almost never meet outside this time. The place itself provides a spectacular 360 degree panorama of beauty. To the west lie the soft undulating hills towards Connemara, the baby hills which eventually lead to the higher and much grander Twelve Pins. To the south is the Atlantic with the three Aran Islands lying low on the horizon. The soft outline of the Burren, that place of stony barren soil, lies just to the east of the islands, the gray limestone visible across the bay. To the north is open bog land and small lakes dotting the purple rust coloured bog. Not a house to be seen anywhere, in fact nothing but open sea, open country, the only sounds the occasional bird flying overhead, the soft drip of a bog stream, the wind gusting across the hillside. The air is clear in this elevated road, the silence awesome. We wave to the occasional person saving their own turf which needs to be banked and dried before carrying it home for winter fires. An hour here feels like a day-long spa. We arrive back to our cars, windswept and invigorated, talked out and happy in each other's company. Lorna happens to be a poet and here is her poem, about this place we both love so much, taken from her second collection, *Witness Trees*.

☙ *Walking the Bog Road*

It came to her that happiness would feel like a lark
rising from the pit of her stomach to her head
and explode in a song only she would recognise.

That her heart was a walled garden tended by gardeners
with names like Prudence, Constance and Faith,
but her life bore a closer resemblance to a hilltop bog
and the people in it, eggs laid by song-birds on the ground,
invisible to the human eye yet utterly exposed.

That relationships were all about picking steps
across that bog without disturbing any nests,
and the possibility of joy somehow hung
on an intimacy with frailty only known in wildness;

like the lark's eggs it was something
that could not be grasped, something
eternally to be hatched.

Lorna Shaughnessy ☙

Here is another writer's take on a place she loves: the Pollack holes in Kilkee (notice how writing this memory brings her to another memory of a different place which often happens in this kind of writing). The 'kick the wall' referred to at the end of the piece is a time-honoured tradition while walking the 'prom' in Salthill, Galway.

℘ *A Special Place for Me*

I was walking along the top of the cliffs in Kilkee, fear in my belly as I was up so high. I got down on my knees, onto my stomach and wriggled forward to peer down over the side. There was a long drop below me to the sea where the white waves were crashing against the base of the cliff. The wind blew upwards along the cliff into my face and my head was cleared of its clouds. The seagulls flew below and their screams were blown up to my ears by the wind.

I gently edged back and slowly rose up. The blue sea stretched out in front of me to America. The wind from the West blew through my long hair which streamed out behind me. I felt like I was on top of the world. I was alone, no other walkers on the cliff. The noise of the wind rushed past my ears. My skirt wrapped round my legs, then blew up in the air. I grabbed it and pushed it down.

I meandered back down the narrow path, still enjoying the wonderful feeling of space and freedom as I looked far out to sea along the horizon. Slowly, I walked down towards the Pollack holes. In the deep pools between the sandy coloured rocks, the water looked in parts a turquoise blue and a deep dark brown where there was seaweed. People were walking on the rocks, jumping in and pulling themselves out of the water. I longed to join them but wasn't allowed.

I wandered further down the road, past the B & B where I was staying with my aunts and sister, down along the road towards the beach, looking over at the hotel where my grandparents spent many holidays. Another knot in my stomach.

The sea, blue or grey, has always called me to it. Every Sunday as a teenager, I set out from home to walk to the prom. My favourite day was stormy, the wind full of spray almost blowing me over. It was a battle to walk along the prom into the westerly wind, but the turmoil of the sea and the strength of the wind matched the turmoil inside me. Something I could fight against like a punch bag. But I could also see a long way to the horizon, to the end of the prom, battling down to Blackrock, hiding behind the walls for shelter. Those walls, where as a teenager, I hid, changed into my swimsuit and, along with many others, upset all the men in Men-Only-Blackrock, who grabbed their towels and hid their bodies, thank God! We weren't there to see them but to have the pleasure of diving off the diving tower, fear in our bellies. Edging out to the edge. Jump in. Splash. Legs turn orange with the belly flop. Swim to the raft, swim back from the raft. Dive under; somersault. Feel like a fish, graceful, a porpoise, the water caressing past my skin. Lying on my back, looking at the blue sky swim out again. Swim in and out.

Stormy day, kick the wall, turn, wind pushing me along, into my back. Steady my back against the wind, nearly landing on my face. It will be a shorter journey home. Reach into my pocket, my treat, a Crunchie, breaking off a bit. Crunch, stick to my teeth, savour the sweetness.

Ann Marie Cleere

So, write about a place that soothes you.
Describe the place.
What is it like?
Now write a memory of a time in that place.

Exercise Two: *The Map*

Map or sketch a significant place. It could be a place you spent a lot of time at some stage in your life. Maybe you came to some big decision there. Did being there change you in some way? Did some event of real importance take place there?

Don't worry about the drawing. This is just for you. Let your hand feel the way. Stick with what comes to mind.

Label the places as you recall and draw them. Now write about A Time When...

Exercise Three: *The First House*

Write about the first house you remember. This may be the house you grew up in or it may be a place you spent holidays in.

What was it like?

What sounds do you associate with this house?

In the poem 'The Great Blasket Island' by Julie O'Callaghan six men return to the abandoned home of their birth and remember

> all the nagging and praying
> and scolding and giggling
> and crying and gossiping.

What smells do you remember from this house? The smell of freshly baked bread? The smell of turf burning? Were the rooms full of light or dark?

In the Musee D'Orangerie in Paris, the Monet room was designed especially for his Water Lily paintings which were painted on the circular walls. Though you can take a virtual tour of the room, the quality of the light in the room itself has to be seen to be believed. There is a pinkish hue to it. It's not really like 'looking' at water lily paintings but being actually there with water lilies all around. The paintings suffuse the whole room with their vibrancy, their colour, their stillness. Last summer, I witnessed a stunning dawn of pinks and gold as the sun rose from behind the lighthouse hill on Sherkin Island. The still water of the bay was suffused with pink cloud reflections. The whole transition from an inky star-filled night draining into daylight lasted only a few minutes at most but it was like standing in the Water Lily room in Paris and seeing all the pinks, lilacs and blues cast their colours.

What was the light like in this house you have chosen to write about? Was there a room full of early morning sunlight? Were the windows big and wide or tall and narrow?
Was there a playhouse? A tree house? A hidey hole under the stairs? Often we are drawn to such places as children, to quiet secret places we can slope off to and read a book or daydream.

In his wonderful short story 'The Lumber Room', Saki conjures up an attic to be a place 'of unimaginable treasures'.

Alternatively, you could try writing about a house you wish you'd had or that you would love to have now.
Describe this wonderful place that you have in your mind's eye.
Open the door and describe what you see, touch, hear, smell.

Here the writer returns to a house she spent a lot of time in as a child.

❧ *Nobody is Home*

The gravel crunched under our feet. The white wrought-iron garden gate opened slowly, stiffly – long years of being unused. The tall oaks moved their bare branches in the dark night sky. The roses and clematis lay dormant as their skeletons wound around the arch of the hall door. Warm light flowed out through the delicate glass that fanned over that wooden door. I could feel the thatch sitting snugly on the long farmhouse.

Anne turned the key ... And I stepped back into my childhood. I had a feeling of coming home. The white painted wooden shutters on the sash windows kept out the November blackness. The same carpet going up the stairs, still shiny brass rods holding it in place. Framed pictures of our ancestors, long vacated this plane, were still hanging on the walls. Which one did I look like? What had been passed down to me?

The same creak of the wide, worn, uneven wooden steps leading down to the cool of the bathroom. It has its own particular smell of disinfectant. Smelled elsewhere brought me to this place in an instant. Evoking my child self.

The dining room lay ready, the fire was set. And on the long polished rosewood table lay our letters. Our archive. Every single letter kept! From all nine of us, each one we had written to Nonie and Maggie over a span of fifteen years of our childhoods were waiting for us, bundled into a chronological pile, childish handwriting turning to the more formed teenage script.

A feast of the past. The fire crackled ... we just had to put a match to it and it roared into life. Burning the felled oaks that had protected this farm long ago. Turning to ash. Potash.

The red and black flags in the kitchen, worn from two hundred and seventy-four years of use, were warm under my feet from the loyal Aga, now converted to oil. The dresser with childhood breakfast bowls stood sentry between the two doors leading down to the scullery, one on either side. The long pine table with its form or 'firm' as Maggie pronounced it was under the high kitchen window, bars on this one. And the box was there, smaller looking now.

Here Maggie sat, on this wooden box, each and every night. Not even a cushion under her. Perched here, her back bending with age. Her iron grey hair streaked with black, apron still on. I never saw her in that house without her apron on, the dark blue one with tiny white flowers. In service. Since she was fifteen. Called herself a spinster.

'The right man never came,' she said. Her hands gnarled and twirling with a mind of their own. Old age. Yet it was here we sat and yearned to be, night after night, story after story told. Sucking those Yorkshire toffees. Heaven.

Anne and I, adult selves now, go back into the dining room ... to read. To read our childhood selves detailed accounts of simple events. All starting with 'Dear Nonie and Maggie, I hope you are well...' Puppies, new uniforms, extensions, camping holidays, birthdays, sickness, friendships, games won and lost and hoped for things, wishes. Tears of laughter, things we had completely forgotten. All here. The power of letters still working decades later.

A detailed account of the first Irish college Collette and I went to. How we got stranded in Galway on our way to Inis Thair, off the

coast of our grandmother's town. Edited version, of course. The
station master taking us for runaways. The detail of the large heavy
suitcase, lumped inch by inch all the way to Nuns Island to Granny's
house, safety. Colette's elder sister fury at me for not cooperating
with the station master. Her 'I thought we were going to be arrested!'
Hilarious stuff. Laughing at the younger me.

Making our way upstairs, down the long, low corridor, shorter
now? And stepping down into our childhood bedroom of our
summers at this golden fruit farm in Co. Meath. A long, long way
from Limerick, no phone, only rare letters home. Chamber pots
under the beds, potties because it was too long, too dark to make
your way to the bathroom down below in the dead of the night. The
beds, brass knobs at each corner of the iron bedsteads. Beds tucked
under the eaves, no square rooms, but irregular – like life. Brass bed,
huge and regal only in the Great Grandmother's bedroom. In our
room 'there are four corners on my bed. There are four angels wings
outspread...' Angel on each corner. Have they stayed with me all my
life? Angel gazing gently with her wonderful golden halo down at me
from the wall.

Horsehair mattresses. Duck down eiderdowns, plum sateen, huge
and comforting on top of blankets and starched linen sheets. Back
then we slipped in to coolness, till your toes meet the hot rubber of
the hottie, your hot water bottle, just yours, placed here by Maggie.
We would be just after an hour on our knees, peeping through the
back of the chair. Reciting the rosary by the fire in the dining room.
All called together, no exceptions, beads playing in our tiny hands.
Nonie, Maggie and us girls. Holy Mary mother of God, pray for us
sinners. Stretched hour. Going on and on. Nonie sprinkling us with
cool holy water as we trudge up the stairs. Released. Getting lighter
all the time till we can race down the unlit corridor to our room.
Freed.

Now, Anne and I, back in our childhood beds, can't sleep a wink.
Wind howls outside the night-lit window. Relics, Holy Marys stare
at us from every available surface. Unnerving. Pictures of Dad frozen

as a seven year old, in cricket whites ... another time. A boy we did not know.

We imagine and feel our ancestral spirits flit through us all night. A night that over one hundred years ago Great Grandmother Thomasina walked the rooms in labour with Nonie. Her first born. Her heir in a matriarchal system, the men moved aside. Her unmarried sisters nursing attendance. For it would have been her birthday today. Nonie's birthday. We feel it, though not know it till later. We are in a waking dream; yet when morning light chinks in through the shutters, I hear it. An echo: 'You are always being looked after, you are special.'

Perhaps this was what I came to this childhood place to remember now.

Triona Byrne

Exercise Four: *A Building I Love*

There was a stage in my life when, accompanied by my first baby wrapped snugly in a buggy, I spent a whole lot of time in the Botanical Gardens in Glasnevin. It's a pretty stupendous place, full of small oases of calm. The Palm House was a particularly exotic location, dark and mysterious and, on the coldest of winter days, wonderfully hot and humid. It was like stepping into another world. I still remember the drip of water, the still silence of the place, its aroma of damp and greenery, the scent of the Orchid House, the sense of light and dark from the tall trees growing there, what is called 'the cluttered green jungle worn by time' in a recently published book of photographs of the Palm House by Amelia Stein.

Describe a building you love, using all your senses: the smells, the sounds, the sights, the atmosphere.
When do you go there?
What does it mean to you?

Here the writer describes a pretty unusual 'building' he loves.

❧ *The Haircut-Donegal Mobile Barber, 2011*

The suspension groans and mildly squeaks,
the old van's door protests and creaks,
I enter,
I am in and just in time.

The floor sags, I pick my seat,
clippings and tissues around my feet,
the Racing Post, old betting slips,
with total focus, Eamon clips.

Mohamad Ali adorns the wall,
boxing lessons in the village hall,
the gent in the chair is thin of hair,
So, beckoned, I take the welcome seat,
ready for my monthly treat.

The chair is warm, springs taut within,
the leather old and wafer thin,
relax, enjoy, inhale the smoke,
NO SMOKING sign is just a joke.

The towel is tight around my neck,
the soap, the razor and scissors check,
relax, enjoy the minutes here,
as Eamon snips from ear to ear.

His chat, his jokes, his observations,
enjoyed by all denominations,
his garden stories loved by all,
and anecdotes they just enthral.

Reflected through the mirrors glass,
clients as pupils in the barber's class.
Weather, wind and other things,
visitors, family and the joy they bring,

the news, the footie and the GAA
taxation, bankers and who will pay
the Royal visit, the Dali Lama,
cattle prices and – yes – Obama,

who's getting married and who has passed,
price of houses, will it last,
all discussed in Eamon's chair.
Fountain of knowledge as he cuts our hair.

How's that? I hear. I take a look,
annoyed how little time it took.
I pay my shearer, shake his hand,
and leave the barber's, looking grand.

Twill be a month till I return,
the court, the chat and friends adjourn.
A sneaky look in Centra's door
confirms a haircut to adore.

Iain Mac Clean

In the next chapter, we look at childhood, where all story telling begins. Childhood is always a rich store of memory from which to write and in using the voice of our childhood self, we can go back to far away times and tell the story anew.

7

Childhood

When people are given writing exercises about their childhood, their adolescence and, especially when they are asked to use the voice and the words of whatever age they are writing about, their writing usually becomes alive with the moment they are recalling. It is as if, when they are reading their work, that the older person who is sitting at the table reading is not there at all and, in her or his place, is an anxious five-year-old on his way to school for the first time or an excited teenager getting ready for her first dance. This happens especially when people write in the first person 'I' using the language of their childhood, phrases, nicknames, all of which help to bring the memory back vividly.

The childhood we each hold in our head is a crucial part of how we make sense of our lives. Sometimes if the story we tell ourselves about our childhood is very negative it can trap us. We endlessly repeat the same lines to ourselves; we seem forever caught as if in a very dense wood. We can't see a way forward. In all of us, there is the child part, the little person who still perhaps feels she didn't get a break or felt put down. Even if our childhood was a happy one, there are moments we can easily recall of feeling miserable or put out by events. Writing offers a chance to revisit events and can help us to work out our feelings about these times from our younger years. If the memories which come floating to the surface are difficult to deal with, take it all at your own pace, look for support if you think you need it.

Exercise One: *First Days*

Roger McGough, the Liverpool poet, has written a wonderful and gently humorous poem of a first day at school using the voice of a four- or five-year-old. The child hears all these new words, misinterpreting most of them; classrooms become 'glass rooms', teachers are people 'who make the tea'. He has forgotten his name and hopes it is sewn on somewhere.

For this exercise, write a memory from childhood/adolescence using the voice of the child/teenager at that age. Conjure up how it actually felt to be you in that new experience. It could be your first day at school, it could be a happy or a sad memory. It could be your first experience of death when a grandparent died or the day your new baby sister came home from the hospital; it could be a day you first went on a train or to the cinema for the first time.

Like other exercises in this book, try to remember using all your sense memories of that event: the sounds of the play yard, the smell of the new uniform. So now write about some first moment in your life that you recall vividly.

Exercise Two: *My Favourite Toy*

Think of a favourite childhood toy. Everybody's got one. I can still vividly conjure up the bald head of Geraldine, my doll who accompanied me on all my childhood adventures from the age of three. My sister's doll was far prettier with blond curls but Geraldine had rosy cheeks and eyes that opened and shut and, most importantly, she could actually cry. I loved her dearly and even when her arms were practically torn out of their sockets, and there was a hole in her back where her battery had fallen out, silencing her crying forever, I still dragged her around after me. Dolls, teddy bears, stuffed animals are the silent witnesses who accompany us on all our adventures, good and bad.

In this exercise switch your viewpoint on whatever event you recall from your childhood and write a memory about that event from the viewpoint of your particular favourite toy beginning with the words: I remember when...

Exercise Three: *Teenage Kicks*

John Peel, the BBC Radio One DJ, rated the 1978 song *Teenage Kicks* by the Undertones as his all time favourite song so much so that he said he'd like the opening line 'teenage dreams so hard to beat' on his tombstone. There is something incredibly wild at heart about being a teenager with dreams that nobody has yet punctured. Look back on early interviews with bands like The Beatles and you see in their faces and in their wide-eyed good humour that same sort of self-belief.

What sucks is that teenage dreams do get punctured: 'What hurts so much about youth isn't the actual butt whippings the world delivers. It's the stupid hopes playacting like certainties.' (Mary Karr, *Lit: A Memoir*)

But even when dreams are shattered and the world seems to be falling apart, people are capable of acts of wonderful defiance. One of the most evocative moments in the film *The Dead Poets Society* is when the teacher, played by Robin Williams, returns to his beloved classroom to collect his things. He is in disgrace but here was where he made literature come alive for this group of boys. He made them see that they could follow their dreams. As he leaves, one boy stands on his desk and shouts 'Oh Captain, my captain', followed by another and then another until all of the boys are standing in defiance of the school principal.

We all have moments when we want to rebel. Fleur Adcock expresses the rebellious defiance of teenagers perfectly in the following poem.

᠁ *For Heidi with Blue Hair*

When you dyed your hair blue
(or at least, ultramarine
for the clipped sides, with a crest
of jet black spikes on top)
you were sent home from school

because, as the headmistress put it,
although dyed hair was not
specifically forbidden, yours,
was, apart from anything else,
not done in the school colours.

Tears in the kitchen, telephone calls
to school from your freedom-loving father;
'She's not a punk in her behaviour;
It's just a style.' (You wiped your eyes,
Also not in a school colour.)

'She discussed it with me first –
We checked the rules.' 'And anyway, Dad
it cost twenty-five dollars.
Tell them it won't wash out –
Not even if I wanted to try.'

It would have been unfair to mention
your mother's death, but that
shimmered behind the arguments
The school had nothing else against you;
the teachers twittered and gave in.

Next day your black friend had hers done
in grey, white and flaxen yellow –
the school colours precisely;
an act of solidarity, a witty
tease. The battle was already won.

Fleur Adcock

Here the writer describes her own 'Heidi' moment, which occurred, as it happens, as an adult.

A Time When I Didn't Conform

My whole life was spent obeying, behaving, reacting, worrying, conforming, believing. I grew up in a house of rules and regulations, black and white, controlled by church. These rules ordered me into a career that wasn't me, into a marriage where I was stifled, into a way of life that held me firmly imprisoned in the pressure of 'getting it right'. Eventually I did break free from that place but continued to study, to work, to give good example, to behave myself. And then one summer I went to Connemara on holiday. I rented a house on the Sky Road, took some time from work and enjoyed every minute. Summer's end came and the responsible me was preparing to head back to 'AA Roadwatch' Dublin and the sensible job. Something snapped. In a flash of clarity I decided, no, I'm not going. This is where I want to be. So I stayed!

Úna McKeever

Write about a time when you had a 'Heidi' moment in your own life. It might not have been when you were a teenager. It could be anytime at all.
Who was there?
What happened?
What was the outcome?
What did you learn?
If you can't think of one, then write about a moment you wish you had rebelled but didn't. What stopped you?

Exercise Four: Names

We often have baby names we were called in childhood, names that perhaps only our immediate family used. Or you might have been teased at school with a nickname or perhaps you loved the nickname you acquired. Some names are automatically shortened. Siblings might tease with a particular version of your name or call you something else entirely. Parents often have their own special pet names for small children, names that can sometimes be used for much longer than childhood.

Make a list of all the names you were called in childhood, then pick one and start writing.
Who called you this name?
What did you think of the name?
When did you stop using it or having it used by other people?

Exercise Five: *Writing Your Own Song*

Janis Ian's evocative song 'When I Was Seventeen' strikes a chord with a lot of people because it evokes the awkwardness of adolescence and how we can feel so adrift.

Write your own song/poem/short piece beginning with the evocative song title: When I Was Seventeen...

OR

Write that sentence three or four times down the left hand side of the page and then finish each sentence. Do this without trying too hard, without thinking too much about what you're going to write.
So, for example:

> When I was seventeen, I fell in love with...
>
> When I was seventeen, I flunked out of school and...
>
> When I was seventeen I won a medal at...

The repetitive rhythm of these lines might surprise you in terms of what you remember.

Exercise Six: *Stories From Your Family*

You know how it is. There's a big family gathering, the first in quite a while. It's getting late but nobody wants to leave because you've reached that stage in proceedings where the warm glow of reminiscence has fallen upon the assembled family members as people swap story after story. My husband and his brothers like to recall a trip taken from Lagos to Liverpool by liner when they were children. Once on board, the boys quickly grew bored with activities on the upper decks and, to their great delight, found a group of caged monkeys during one of their forays into the bowels of the ship. Unknown to their exhausted mother, they spent the rest of the voyage helpfully feeding them with scraps from the dining table. The monkeys arrived in Liverpool destined for their new home in a zoo in a morbidly obese condition.

Families tend to have such stories in spades. Of course, there is every possibility that proceedings may well descend into that other great institution, the family row, as everyone gives their own version of events. We all love to hear those stories though. They give us a sense of being part of a larger family.

One of a growing trend of television programmes on the theme of exploring genealogy currently doing the rounds is called *Who do you think you are?* – and there's even a celebrity version. What all the participants have in common is a burning desire to know who they really are; the story not only of their own immediate family but the story of their family going back over several generations and often, particularly with Irish families, where emigration has been involved, across two continents. We want to trace the connections down through the generations of our own tribe, see how it all fits together, make sense of our story and that is exactly what happens on the programme. People see the narrative of their family unfold on one or both sides of the family tree. They are often surprised, amazed, shocked and saddened by what they find but they are never bored by their history. It is fascinating because it is their story, the story of their people.

And knowing about our larger family is good for us, as research psychologists Marshall Duke and Robyn Fivush at the Emory University Family Narratives Project have found. In their research they found that children who knew more about their family history were better adjusted and more resilient with a strong belief in their capacity to control things that happened to them. Having a strong 'intergenerational self' is good for children and for everyone else too, knowing that we belong to something bigger than ourselves.

So how do families pass on these stories? The researchers found that stories tended to be transferred mainly by mothers and grandmothers and were typically told at mealtimes, holidays and other family gatherings. In a recent blog Marshall Dukes pointed out that it is not the content of what is known that is the critical factor, but the process by which these things came to be known: 'In order to hear family stories, people need to sit down with one another and not be distracted. Some people have to talk and some have to listen. The stories need to be told over and over and the times of sitting together need to be multiple and occur over many years.'

And now, looking at your own family, if there was only one story that you could tell about your past/your own history or that of your family, what would that story be?

You may have heard this story a hundred times or perhaps only once. Recall the words that were used, the language, the names of people, places. Try to be as exact as possible. Imagine you are the person charged with recording this story for posterity and it's up to you to get it right.

And onwards to the endlessly interesting theme of relationships; from parents to children, friends and lovers. In the next chapter we get to explore how we feel about them.

8

People: Writing About Relationships

In the story of our own lives, other people play their roles, some with bit parts, a walk-on role that may or may not have much significance in our story, others have huge roles. Our family of origin, our partners, our children, friends, a wonderful teacher, a kind colleague, any or all of these may have had a strong influence on our story or at least how we see it.

In a long-term therapeutic writing group, the people who inhabit the writings of the participants often begin to reappear. The effect is almost a feeling that there are other people present, much-loved mentors, great teachers, trusted friends, mourned grandparents. They come and go through the writing of the group. Sometimes the writing expresses sadness, anger, hurt, grief. Sometimes these people get to speak for themselves through dialogue exercises when the writer switches viewpoint and lets the person speak for themselves. In all of this writing what can happen is a reworking of painful stories. Writing and reading back allows for a breathing space, a time to reflect, even to hear other people's reactions to an event which has been recounted.

The exercises here give you an opportunity to look at different relationships of significance in your life and I've included quite a few to give you some choices in relation to whom or what you write about.

Sometimes the best way to write about sadness or anger to do with particular people from our lives is to write slant/to write in an oblique way, not meeting the pain or sense of loss head on but rather sideways. This can help us express what may have seemed inexpressible before. In the exercise that follows, that is what happens, through looking at the objects that belong to someone, we discover a lot about the person.

Exercise One: *My Mother's Handbag*

In the poem by Ruth Fainlight, 'My Mother's Handbag', she sums up what her mother's life was about through a careful and loving examination of her handbag. Female readers will probably immediately identify with this idea. A woman's handbag does say something about her life.

It can be poignant to watch the way in which elderly women 'mind' their handbags. So much of our lives can be in other people's gift as we approach old age but handbags and their contents still express something very vital about us.

Here is one writer's response to the exercise of describing her mother's handbag.

✍ My Mother's Handbag

It went everywhere with her. It was made of black leather with an ornate twist clasp. The handles were short but sturdy. It was like a part of Mammy's anatomy, located somewhere between her elbow and her chest wall. A cursory examination of it would provide many clues to her life. However, it proved difficult to extricate it from her person. About once a month the conversation was initiated by me. 'Mam, are you carrying a lot of cash in your bag?' Her reply was always in the negative, 'No very little. I'll need some cash this week.' After a bit of persuasion the bag was eventually handed over to count and lodge the money that had accumulated since the last inventory.

This ritual happened on a monthly basis. The handbag was emptied, out tumbled the Silvermints usually in ones, the rosary beads, loose change, the pension book, some dog-eared letters, photos, a lace-trimmed handkerchief, ten Silk Cut and, of course, much more cash than she had realised. Every birthday or Christmas, a new handbag was given as a present. This was graciously received only to take its place with all the others on the top of the wardrobe. The old leather bag was comfortable and held all the memories.

It started life as an accessory to be worn with the good suit going to town and to weddings and funerals. As time went on though, it became much more than that. It was the familiar friend, the constant companion, the keeper of memories, the symbol of a life well lived. The bag went to the doctors' appointments, the hospital for the tests, with the appointment letter carefully stored in the zip pocket. When she got the first small stroke the bag was found beside her on the ground. Gradually her health worsened and even sometimes she forgot about the bag. This was a worrying sign. When each of us in turn squeezed her hand and told her it was okay to go, that we were all there and she could now depart in peace, the bag was consigned to the bedside locker.

After her funeral we thought of the bag and we all shed a tear when the bag was opened and the familiar smell of 4711 cologne wafted out. They had been separated at last.

Breeda O'Connor 🐾

Write about your own mother's handbag.
If she didn't use one then why not write about some other possession of importance to her?

Exercise Two: *Fathers*

Poetry can be a wonderful way to explore the theme of relationships since so many wonderful poems have been written on the theme of parenting, family, friendship, love. When I work with groups, I often read two poems that express brilliantly in each case the relationship between the poets and their fathers: Michael Davitt's 'An Scathán' ('The Mirror') translated from the original Irish by Paul Muldoon and *Those Winter Sundays* by Robert Hayden. Both poems depict a sort of unarticulated love between fathers and sons which is best expressed in actions.

In the following example, the writer provided her own introduction to the poem she wrote in response to an exercise on writing on the theme of fathers.

ℬ *Celebration*

When my father was diagnosed with terminal lung cancer, my four siblings and I rallied around our parents to support and be supported. After several intense and sad days, I returned to my own home and immediately felt the need to go outdoors and walk the openness of our country road, ironically named the Dark Road. As I walked, in denial, I refused to think of the future without him as being sad and negative, and defiantly searched for 'signs'. I didn't have to search far as the wonders of nature below happened on that walk. Dad, Gerard O'Leary, died on December 30, 2010, one month after I started chemotherapy for breast cancer.

I will celebrate my Father
Walk bird-singing paths
Where the low-flying magpie skims stone walls
Where wrens and finches weave and skip
Avoiding his furtive dives

I will celebrate my Father
Breathe the clean, crisp air
As the cold Spring chills my cheeks
Burns my stinging fingers
As the breeze blows my hair

I will celebrate my Father
By spying smiling first daffodils
Young and yellow with pale green fronds

Bubbling from a bank of new holly
Capped by four swans taking flight from the turlach

I will celebrate my Father
When soft crunching branches on the mossy wood floor
Grow into brown fur ponies staring out and lonely
Wanting company from the brighter road
When I swallow, sigh and smile

I will celebrate my Father
By speaking these lines
By teasing out sounds and stroking rhymes
By conducting my meagre orchestra of letters, thoughts
And unsung words, not being a chorister like him

When soon he will not touch me, see me, hear me,
And I will look for him on my walk,
Will that magpie flight be enough? The calling swans?
Will the new growth be his delight? The air his sound?
Will it celebrate the gentle man?
Will he be near me, will he give me a sign?

Marion Cox

Now write a memory of your own father.
What was he like?
Write about a specific time when...

Exercise Three: *Using Your Senses to Describe and Remember*

Think of a person you know well.
Write a list of any or all of these that you associate with them:

- a colour/a type of clothing.
- an object: a natural thing (for example, a flower); a tool (for example, spanner); a book they loved; perhaps a handbag.

- ❧ a smell, odour, fragrance (the smell of tobacco, for example).

- ❧ music/singing or something they habitually said.

- ❧ a particular taste (Granny's apple pie).

- ❧ a physical sense (warmth, shivery, irritated, serene).

- ❧ texture or tactile sense.

- ❧ any sixth-sense feeling (a feeling of safety/a feeling of fear).

Now write about a time you remember with that person.

Exercise Four: *Giving and Receiving Advice*

> In my younger and more vulnerable years my father gave me some
> advice that I've been turning over in my mind ever since.
>
> F. Scott Fitzgerald, *The Great Gatsby*

Write about a good piece of advice you received and followed.

Or write about a piece of advice you received and ignored.

Or try writing a piece of advice you would like to give to someone in your life right now.

Or if you're feeling particularly stuck, you might like to imagine having a conversation with your own inner wise self (what does your wise self look like?). Now imagine your inner wise self gives you some advice: what is this advice?

Exercise Five: *I Carry In My Heart...*

We all carry different people in our hearts, people whom we think about, wonder about, miss when they are gone and most of all love. The poem by E. E. Cummings from which this exercise title is taken is a love poem about the person he carries in his heart.

Who do you carry with you in your heart? Begin writing with the words: I carry you in my heart...

Exercise Six: *My Hero*

Think of someone who has had a big influence on your life.
Describe the moment you met that important person for the first time.
Begin your piece with the words: I'll never forget when I met...
What were the circumstances? What was your initial impression of that person and did it change later?
How did you feel?

Exercise Seven: *Letter of Forgiveness*

Writing unsent letters can be a wonderful way of getting things off our chests.

Think of a resentment you have harboured; someone who makes you angry just thinking about them; someone who hurt you.
Now try writing a letter (unsent) of forgiveness to that person.

Exercise Eight: *Buoyed Up*

At one stage in my life, I lived in a wonderful square in Dublin. My constant companions during all those years were three friends who all had children around the same age. In summer we used to spend long days out in the Hole in the Wall beach in Howth. It was in many ways a magical time but being at home with small children, no matter what way you cut it, can be tough. You can feel lonely, bored, adrift from life. You begin to wonder why are you doing this. What I found with my friends, who also happened to be my neighbours, was a deep friendship that meant that, when any one of us was having a particularly tough time of it, the others would cheer them along. We buoyed each other up.

Write about someone who buoyed you up when you were stressed or going through a difficult time. It could be a cheerful driver on the bus you get every morning to work. He greets you with a smile and you feel immediately better.

Describe a time in your life when you were buoyed up. Who did this for you? Or describe a time when you buoyed someone else up. What did it feel like to do that?

Exercise Nine: *Retrouvaille*

A recent trawl through www.stumbleupon.com threw up an interesting webpage which listed ten words to describe relationships that don't appear in the English language. One of these was the French word *retrouvaille* meaning rediscovery, the happiness of meeting again after a long time.

Have you ever met someone again after a long time?
Have you ever rediscovered the joy of being with someone you used to love spending time with? Or have you daydreamed about this meeting?

One very useful way of doing this exercise and a way which may surprise you is to recount this imaginary meeting as a dialogue. Conversations with people, real or imaginary, allow us to explore issues. Dialogues can be with people we know, people we don't know but wish we did or people now dead.

Now think of someone you have got to know again, to rediscover.
Describe the moment of reunion; if it hasn't happened then imagine that it has.
What was it like? Use all your senses. 'I was sitting waiting in a cafe. The sun was streaming in the window...'
What happened then?

Exercise Ten: *Changing Viewpoint*

A central factor in the success of psychotherapy is that people attain a better sense of perspective on their lives, an ability to stand back more and look at things from different perspectives. The journal *Human Relations* produced a special edition in 2012 focused on sense-making and storytelling. One paper by Whittle and Muller examined the way people told each other stories about the financial crisis. The authors analysed the stories constructed by bankers during a public hearing of the Treasury Select Committee in the UK and their analysis, not surprisingly, highlights two competing storylines. In Storyline One, the committee members view the bankers as villains who brought down the world and as immoral and greedy, while the bankers in Storyline Two believe they are victims of a 'financial tsunami'. The moral plot line depends on your viewpoint.

Every year or so, a group of my old school friends meet for dinner. We all went to secondary school together and have been friends ever since. One year recently we got to talking about our old Alma Mater, something we had never discussed as a group before. I was very struck by how different our viewpoints were on the same set of experiences. Some people had adored every moment of that time, loved most of the teachers and thought it was a great school. Others didn't agree, had found the whole place a little stifling, the teaching at times not so great. It all depended on the point of view.

Switching point of view is perhaps one of the best exercises you can do in therapeutic writing. The more you stay within your own head, your own prejudices, the more self-fulfilling they become. Without even being conscious of it, you automatically filter out any information that might debunk your viewpoint.

The artist Raghava KK is a self-taught artist recently named by CNN as one of ten remarkable people the world has yet to know about. He has developed a unique illustrated children's book for the iPad which ostensibly is about potty training but when the iPad is shaken the characters all change; the heterosexual couple become a lesbian couple; shake it again and they become a homosexual couple. Raghava was brought up in a very multicultural way with experience of all religions in India. From an early age he got used to having to see things from other people's viewpoint. He maintains that the key to overcoming bias is to be able to separate fact from the bias of your own perspective. Now with children of his own he says: 'The only way to teach children creativity is to teach them to switch perspective. I can't promise my child a life without bias but I promise to bias my child with multiple perspectives.' Part of that skill of changing perspectives is taught in his iPad story which literally shakes the story up and forces the reader to see things differently.

In our relationships we often get bogged down with the limited viewpoint we have. We filter all the information we receive through the lenses of our own prejudices. So we see someone as lazy and uncooperative and the examples of this laziness and lack of cooperation are everywhere. They are everywhere because it's all we're prepared to see.

This phenomenon is often captured on camera in television programmes like *Super Nanny*. The parents are at the end of their tether, have tried everything. Nothing works. What happens in the intervention is that they take a different view of things, especially in looking for good behaviour, to catch their children being good and reinforcing that and not just spend their time looking for more bad behaviour to punish. The results often make for eye-opening television as hitherto unmanageable children become calm and happy. Likewise, in couples or family therapy, people get to hear what it's like to live with someone like themselves, how their behaviour affects other people.

Now we're going to try shaking your story up a bit in the way that Raghava KK advocates in his wonderful talk on www.ted.com.

Firstly, try writing from the viewpoint of someone who has an utterly opposing view to you on a subject that matters to you both.

Now try writing from the viewpoint of an inanimate object in your life. This object has a more neutral viewpoint on events and it would be interesting to hear what they have to say: a mug on your desk, a painting on the wall, the kitchen clock. So let the clock tell the story of that row you had with your teenage son this morning or record any other event of note that it happened to witness.

Exercise Eleven: Giving Your Heart

This exercise is similar in intent to the earlier one in Chapter Five on the theme of diving in. Its aim is to examine a time when you gave your heart completely to someone/something.

In the poem 'Never Give all the Heart', Yeats advises, based on his own heartbreak with Maude Gonne, not to give all the heart, but it's the people who are prepared to throw caution to the wind and follow their dreams who seem to live life fully. In his famous address at Stanford University commencement, Steve Jobs urged the listening graduates 'to stay hungry, stay foolish'.

So, describe a time when you gave all your heart to someone, something, some ideal.
How did it all work out?
Describe a time when you followed Yeats's advice and held back. How did that work out for you?

And in the next chapter we come to one of the most widely used tools in therapeutic writing: the metaphor, which provides us with a fresh perspective on any situation.

9

Writing Slant: Metaphor

Metaphor is intrinsic to our world. In his book, *I is an Other*, James Geary shows that metaphors are not rhetorical frills at the edges of how we think – they are the very heart of it.

What then is a metaphor? It's a figure of speech in which a situation is compared to a thing although it is not actually that particular thing: 'All the world's a stage.'

In an address on www.ted.com in 2009, Geary states that metaphor lives a secret life all around us. We utter about six metaphors a minute but perhaps mostly are unaware that language is shaping the way we see the world. Metaphor, as a central part of our language, therefore colours everything.

Using the words of Elvis Presley, Geary demonstrates the descriptive power of metaphor: lips are 'volcanoes', love is being 'all shook up'. Similarly, Shakespeare calls Juliet 'the sun'. It's not that she is like the sun; she *is* the sun and this is a vivid and striking description of her importance to Romeo. His world literally revolves around her.

George Lakoff and Mark Johnson have researched the type of metaphors we use in different situations: food metaphors for ideas ('half baked', 'digesting' facts); war metaphors for argument (incidentally war metaphors are often used in the 'fight' against cancer). For money, we often use liquid metaphors 'dipping into savings', 'sponging off friends'.

In an article in the *New York Times*, David Brooks quotes psychologist Michael Morris that when the stock market is going up, we tend to use agent metaphors, implying the market is a living thing with clear intentions. We say the market 'climbs' or 'soars' or 'fights its way upward'. When the market goes down, on the other hand, we use object metaphors, implying it is inanimate. The market 'falls', 'plummets' or 'slides'.

Similarly, in describing any kind of psychological change such as might happen through therapy, people often use the metaphor of a journey, of being on a metaphorical 'road': 'I started out feeling very depressed/anxious/confused ... then I turned a corner/reached a crossroads/changed direction and realised that ... after that I felt more clear headed/less anxious.' In relationships we often define the end point as 'we have reached the end of the road' or 'there's nowhere else to go'.

Metaphor in therapeutic writing helps us write slant, to take a fresh perspective on an event, a person. So metaphor shakes things up. It helps us view things afresh and is probably one of the most useful tools in therapeutic writing. Keeps the mind shaking and rolling as Geary says.

Exercise One: *Behind the Lines*

In this first exercise, we are going to use the analogy of a fight as described by the boxer Mohammed Ali to look at issues we may have faced in our own lives.

> The fight is won or lost far away from witnesses – behind the lines, in the gym, and out there on the road, long before I dance under those lights.
>
> *Muhammad Ali* 🥊

Have you ever spent time behind the lines, in the gym or on the road preparing to do something? It could have been physical preparation for something like a race or a marathon. Or it could have been something like writing a thesis or even a book: long hours hunched over a keyboard before you submit your essay or term paper. Any interview with a highly successful person reveals how much of their life has been spent 'behind the lines' preparing, practising, becoming. Nothing comes easy they say. Hours and hours of work go into that moment where you shine.

In a stunning talk available on www.ted.com Randy Pausch, an American professor of computer science and human–computer interaction and design at Carnegie Mellon University in Pittsburgh, Pennsylvania, gave one last lecture at Carnegie Mellon when he was dying of pancreatic cancer. In it he talked about how it was through relentless hard work that he got to achieve his dreams. He said that he was often asked by students how come he was able to get tenure as a professor a year early. He said, 'Call me any Friday night at ten o'clock in my office and I'll tell you.'

So, for you, what was it like to be behind the lines?
And what was it like to finally dance under the lights?

Exercise Two: *The Oak Tree*

> The strongest oak of the forest is not the one that is protected from the storm and hidden from the sun. It's the one that stands in the open where it is compelled to struggle for its existence against the winds and rains and the scorching sun.
>
> *Napoleon Hill (1883–1970)*

Describe a time when you stood in the open, perhaps alone and struggled against difficulties and became stronger.

Exercise Three: *The Solitaire*

The times we are living through often make us feel like we have no control or power anymore. Everything is happening to us. Similarly when people experience illness they often feel like all control is taken away. It is important to remember and honour times when we were brave and courageous in our lives: When we fought like tigers to protect something important to us; When we were lionhearted; When we were David against Goliath.

The documentary film, *The Pipe*, tells the story of a small Erris community in north Mayo which stood up to the might of Shell Oil (whatever your views on this protest, the film makes for riveting viewing). One scene in the film is of a fisherman heading out to sea to meet the *Solitaire*, a giant ship which would lay the pipe to bring the oil ashore. This man's family had fished on this particular fishing ground for three generations. His lobster pots were positioned where Shell wanted to lay their pipe. The whole fishing community took to sea in a flotilla and protested against the laying of the pipe in that area. Shell then negotiated with each of the fishermen and the next time they went out to protest against the arrival of the enormous ship, the *Solitaire*, there was only the boat of the man who had led the protest and his son's boat. They sailed out alone to face the *Solitaire*.

All of us at sometime have felt like we were facing a *Solitaire* of our own, something much bigger than us. Maybe you felt forced to fight for one of your children who might have needed some special help in school. Maybe you felt that something unfair was happening where you work and you were prepared to take on the system.

List the events in your life where you had to face a *Solitaire* and stand up for something.
What was the *Solitaire* you faced?
Who, if anyone, was in your 'flotilla'?
What was the outcome?

Exercise Four: No Man's Land

The following is an extract from an eyewitness account by Frank Richards, a British soldier, of that famous encounter between the two opposing armies of German and British troops on Christmas Eve, 1914. The spontaneous truce that occurred on that evening and went on through the following day (Christmas Day) is seen as a symbolic moment of peace and humanity in a very brutal war.

❧ *Christmas in the Trenches, 1914*

On Christmas morning we stuck up a board with 'A Merry Christmas' on it. The enemy had stuck up a similar one. Platoons would sometimes go out for twenty-four hours' rest – it was a day at least out of the trench and relieved the monotony a bit — and my platoon had gone out in this way the night before, but a few of us stayed behind to see what would happen. Two of our men then threw their equipment off and jumped on the parapet with their hands above their heads. Two of the Germans did the same and commenced to walk up the river bank, our two men going to meet them. They met and shook hands and then we all got out of the trench.

Buffalo Bill [the Company Commander] rushed into the trench and endeavoured to prevent it, but he was too late: the whole of the Company were now out, and so were the Germans. He had to accept the situation, so soon he and the other company officers climbed out too. We and the Germans met in the middle of no man's land. Their officers were also now out. Our officers exchanged greetings with them. One of the German officers said that he wished he had a camera to take a snapshot, but they were not allowed to carry cameras. Neither were our officers.

We mucked in all day with one another. They were Saxons and some of them could speak English. By the look of them their trenches were in as bad a state as our own. One of their men, speaking in English, mentioned that he had worked in Brighton for some years and that he was fed up to the neck with this damned war and would be glad when it was all over. We told him that he wasn't the only one that was fed up with it. We did not allow them in our trench and they did not allow us in theirs.

The German Company Commander asked Buffalo Bill if he would accept a couple of barrels of beer and assured him that they would not make his men drunk. They had plenty of it in the brewery. He accepted the offer with thanks and a couple of their men rolled the barrels over and we took them into our trench. The German officer sent one of his men back to the trench, who appeared shortly after carrying a tray with bottles and glasses on it. Officers of both sides clinked glasses and drank one another's health. Buffalo Bill had presented them with a plum pudding just before. The officers came to an understanding that the unofficial truce would end at midnight. At dusk we went back to our respective trenches.

The two barrels of beer were drunk, and the German officer was right: if it was possible for a man to have drunk the two barrels himself he would have bursted before he had got drunk. French beer was rotten stuff.

Just before midnight we all made it up not to commence firing before they did. At night there was always plenty of firing by both sides if there were no working parties or patrols out. Mr Richardson, a young officer who had just joined the Battalion and was now a platoon officer in my company, wrote a poem during the night about the Briton and the Bosche meeting in no man's land on Christmas Day, which he read out to us. A few days later it was published in *The Times* or *Morning Post*, I believe.

During the whole of Boxing Day [the day after Christmas] we never fired a shot, and they the same, each side seemed to be waiting for the other to set the ball a-rolling. One of their men shouted across in English and inquired how we had enjoyed the beer. We shouted back and told him it was very weak but that we were very grateful for it. We were conversing off and on during the whole of the day.

Frank Richards, www.eyewitnesstohistory.com

At some point in your life you may have been in a dispute with someone, a painful stand-off where neither of you was prepared to give an inch. And then one of you did. A peace offering was proffered. The lines of communication were at last reopened.

Have you ever found yourself in no man's land with someone or with more than one person? What was it like? Who offered a peace offering first? What was the outcome?

Exercise Five: *Bridges as Connectors*

The bridge is a powerful metaphor psychologically. As I mentioned earlier, people often describe their journey of change as just that: a journey on a road. The bridge represents something that joins two separate places. It's a place where you literally cross from one place to another, from one world to another. It can be a place of no return.

In your life:
What bridges have you crossed? There are so many metaphorical bridges to cross in life: we talk about moving from childhood to being an adult, getting married, becoming a parent for the first time.
What bridges have you burned?
Did you walk away from someone or someplace or a career? Did you drop out of a course? Did you up sticks and move to another place?
What bridges would you like to build? Maybe you have lost contact with someone in your family, a very old friend, a neighbour with whom there was a falling out at some stage.

Exercise Six: *Up on Your High Horse*

When someone is described as being 'up on a high horse', it means that the person is taking a superior or lofty view of other people or the situation. It implies that a cool standoff has occurred. It also implies that the person on the horse is not communicating very well with anyone, that they have placed themselves above everyone else and not in a good way.

People get on high horses for all kinds of reasons but the stance implies that the person has been offended and is pulling away, saying that they don't want to be any part of this. But being up on a height also implies that the person just might fall off.

Describe an occasion when you were up on your high horse.
What caused you to do that?
How did other people react? What did they say?

How did the situation resolve?

What did you learn?

Was it easy to get back down?

Exercise Seven: *Oh, the Places You'll Go*

In his much-loved book, *Oh, the Places You'll Go*, Dr Seuss describes all the places you might end up on life's journey, places like The Waiting Room, where you might spend a long time waiting around for a yes or a no (fiction writers will know this place very well!). You might have ended up in a 'lurch', feeling stuck and unable to move on.

Like Dr Seuss, the following pages depict a whole series of metaphorical places you can go.

The exercise, which you can return to as often as you like and pick a different place from each page, is to pick a phrase from any one of the pages and just start writing about your own experience of that place. Write about A Time When...

You can also use this list of questions to expand your writing.

What was it like?

How did it feel to be there?

Were you there long?

Were you on your own?

And what happened then?

How did things change?

What is different now?

Landscapes of Our Lives

You'll probably instantly recognise a lot of the places that you have spent time in so pick one that jumps out at you, don't think about it too much and start writing. If you get stuck, look at the list of questions above to further your writing.

- On top of the world.
- On a slippery slope.
- In a canoe without a paddle.
- Over the moon.
- Up on your high horse.
- Down in the dumps.
- Away with the fairies.
- Taking a back seat.
- Around the bend.
- Out of your mind.
- On a sticky wicket.
- In the trenches.
- At the coalface.
- At sea.
- At a crossroads.
- Stuck in a lurch.
- On solid ground.
- Over the top.
- In no man's land.
- Between a rock and a hard place.
- Sitting on the fence.
- Between two stools.
- On your last legs.
- In the Doldrums.
- The wriggle room.
- In the doghouse.

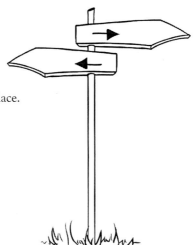

Here's one person's take on 'A Sticky Wicket'.

❦ A Sticky Wicket

The stickiest wicket I have ever sat on was the chair in the Diagnostic Breast Clinic on International Women's Day, 8th March 2011. I went in there cocky as you like to get the result of a biopsy. It was to be a brief interruption of a day in Galway with my friend. I suspected something amiss when I saw a second woman in the room. Even as I write it, I can feel the tension rising in me. I was not ready to hear I had breast cancer.

'What will I tell my children?' was my first question.

I have no idea what the reply was. I went into outer space. My anxiety was for the poor friend who was going to be told this news before he drove me home. I remember drinking tea in Ballinahinch on the way home and going to a movie in Letterfrack that night. I have no idea what I saw.

Reactions to my news varied. My children were silently upset. They never discussed any of it with me but they rallied round me magnificently. Some friends disappeared in fright. Others tried to fix it. Some of the comments were startling!

'Where did you get the cancer'?

'In my breast.'

'That's the best place to get it.'

'You could be worse.'

'Is that your own hair?' shouted from the far side of the supermarket.

'How many sessions of chemo are you having?'

'Four.'

'You're so lucky.'

True friends moved in around me like great big oak trees where I could lean.

I dug out my diary. I marked the surgery dates and chemotherapy dates in and turned my face into the storm. I wanted the tumour gone fast so there was no delay in the first or second surgeries. Barely conscious from the fright of mutilation, the chemotherapy started with hair loss, mouth ulcers, aching joints, blocked tear ducts, nails lifting from their beds and a tiredness that no sleep would ease. This was quickly followed by the endless trips to be radiated under that cold unforgiving machine. Just to be sure, I was told. How sure? Who knows? Today I am cancer free.

This was the toughest lesson of my life. I talked to this cancer all the way through. I asked it why it came, what it wanted to teach me? And it talked back. It told me that there is only today. It has taught me to spend my time and energy with the people who care about me, listen to me, the ones who laugh and cry with me, who don't judge me and who want to travel the same scary journey of self-awareness. I am learning to let the rest go out of my life with my blessing but with no more of my energy. I am learning to pay attention to what I need rather than worrying about what others might think. This cancer has encouraged me to exercise, to get fresh air and to delight in each moment of health and wellbeing. Oh, and by the way, I have learned that grey hair is acceptable, liberating and cost effective!

Úna McKeever

Things We Do
This is an exercise using metaphor to describe ways of being/things we do. Again, pick one and just start writing. Use the list of questions if you get stuck or to come back to at another time.

- Hanging on by your fingernails.
- Running to stand still.
- Following in someone else's footsteps.
- Flying by the seat of your pants.

- Juggling too many balls in the air.
- Reaching for the stars.
- Ploughing your own furrow.
- Losing the run of yourself.
- Not able to see the wood for the trees.
- Diving headlong in.
- Going nowhere fast.
- Heading into the unknown.
- Taking the scenic route.
- Running on empty.
- Sticking your oar in.

Animal Metaphors

We use animal metaphors a lot to describe people. Probably for every metaphor here you could easily assign it to someone you know. You can either use the exercise to think of someone you know who fits one of these metaphors and then start writing about an occasion when the person showed this trait or else use the exercise to think of an occasion when you yourself were as 'stubborn as a mule' or you became the 'dog in the manger'.

Now write about a time when you were:

- Stubborn as a mule.
- In the doghouse.
- Sick as a parrot.
- Quiet as a mouse.
- The dog in the manger.
- The cat who got the cream.
- Lion hearted.
- Clumsy as an elephant.

- ☙ A bull in a china shop.

- ☙ Fighting like a tiger.

- ☙ Like a bear with a sore paw.

- ☙ Throwing the cat among the pigeons.

Here is an example of someone using the metaphor of a tiger, both fierce and calm to describe her relationship to the world at that time in her life.

✑ *The Tiger*

I can feel myself inside the yellow and black Tiger, being carried. Feel myself swaying with each padding step. Inside. Safe. It is as if this all-powerful being carries me. All at once I am it and it is me. One, though separate. I hear her voice, resonating through me rather than with my ears. I hear with my being. I hear, 'Nothing is insurmountable. This earth is for you.' It is.

Now it seems as if the Tiger grows and grows. One leap takes me across the cold, blue Atlantic Ocean. I am with my sisters. Sipping tea. Sunny time. I am here because I am meant to be. The Tiger breathes. Do my sisters see a Tiger or see me the woman?

Then things change and I'm a Tiger on a mountain top, the winds riffle through my tiger hair. I stretch and see all this beauty before me. The earth, the trees, the sky, the sun, all balanced, all in time. I am the Tiger. I stretch out full in a warm sunny patch and let go ... sleep. Become soft and purring. Total ease. No disease.

I can roar. Mouth open, coming from deep within me. Four feet grounded. Show how powerful I am, letting the world know and hear me. The sky can tremble and ground vibrates as my roar sounds. Expanding, as a stone dropped into a deep lake. This roar is the centre. It is terrifying even to me. Coming from me yet it is beyond me. What will happen now I have roared? The roar travels and roams. My vibration changed. Then I can play, rolling, jumping, running ... just for fun. No purpose.

I can see far with my amber eyes. See in distance and time. Gives me perspective in this time of disease. An eagle eye seeing the full picture. No longer the ant scurrying on the newspaper. Just seeing black and white. In this tiger body all clear. Be here now.

Triona Byrne

The Wild West

From John Wayne to Clint Eastwood, we've all been exposed to a huge variety of metaphors from the colourful language of the Western movie.

Why not head out west for this one and describe a situation when you or someone you know played for high stakes or acted like a lone ranger.

- Playing for high stakes.
- The lone ranger.
- Last chance saloon.
- Riding into the sunset.
- New frontiers.
- Showdown.
- Feeling corralled.
- Hitching your wagon to something.
- Putting all your cards on the table.
- Dying with boots on.
- Circling the wagons.
- Going in with all guns blazing.
- Surrounded on all sides.
- Here come the cavalry.
- Staking out the territory.

Weather Metaphors

Maybe it's from living in Ireland where you can easily have four or five different types of weather in the same day, but using weather metaphors seems to come very naturally to us. Our language is replete with such metaphor.

So in this exercise just pick one and start writing about what it means to you.

- It's a case of sink or swim.
- Swamped with the demands.
- Torrents of abuse.
- Waves of sympathy.
- It's raining on my parade.
- Saving for a rainy day.
- In the same boat.
- Drowning in work.

Our Bodies as Metaphor

Our bodies are great sources for metaphor and our language is rich with anatomical metaphors. Pick one that fits/jumps off the page and start writing.

- Lending a hand.
- Putting your foot in it.
- Giving someone a shoulder to lean on.
- Giving the two fingers.
- Being knock-kneed about something.
- Having butterflies in your stomach.
- Holding something in your heart.
- Giving the thumbs up on something.

- Lending an ear.
- Giving someone the glad eye.
- When your lips are sealed.
- Sticking your nose into something.
- Raised eyebrows.
- Having a brass neck.
- Feeling that your back is to the wall.
- Turning a blind eye.
- Turning the other cheek.

Metaphor provides a way of looking at any issue in a different way, loosening up perhaps our preconceptions which would be more to the fore if we wrote about it in a straightforward way.

The next chapter continues with the idea of writing 'slant' by introducing the theme of fairy tale. We are all familiar with them, know them by heart, read them perhaps to our own children hundreds of times. Now we take a tour through the wonderful land of make-believe and in doing so, find ways to write about the everyday in a new way.

10

Once Upon a Time... Using Fairy Tales to Write

Once Upon a Time... It's a phrase that is likely to transport you back in time, opening up the world of imagination and letting it roam to your own childhood, to reading to your own children using the symbols and archetypes of fairy tales. The words evoke something deep. You are going to go on a journey. If you are reading a story book yourself, you will be brought into a fantastical world of princesses, dragons, woods and wicked queens; of castles, hidden treasure and quests. Thousands of times perhaps you have heard these words – Once Upon a Time – as a prequel to a story. You may have known what was to come, that Snow White would wake up and be rescued by the seven dwarfs, that Cinderella would, after all, get to the ball and that the prince would come and find her with the glass slipper. But each time the journey is still an adventure.

They say that there are only seven basic plots in terms of story. But what makes fairy tales so vivid is the use of those archetypes: the wicked stepmother, the beautiful princess, the ugly but kind beast, the carriages, the houses made of chocolate, the woods, the giants, the castles, the near and the faraway lands, the buried treasure.

Using the fairy tale structure is another use of metaphor. It's taking stock characters/archetypes and projecting our own dreams, thoughts and experiences onto them. The fairy tales we read in childhood for the most part involved flat two-dimensional characters. People were either good or very bad. Complex emotional nuances did not get explored. For the most part the good won out, the bad got punished. The endings were predictable.

Ask anyone to begin to write from the words Once Upon a Time and they will begin to write using the familiar archetypes. They may write about situations from their life as it is now or their life in the past. The great thing about using the fairy tale as a motif for writing is that the archetypes enable us to write 'slant'. They become a metaphor to tackle issues in our lives. We can cast people into roles: the good and wicked, the kind and cruel. We can travel to faraway lands. We can basically remove the story from the everyday and write 'on the big screen'. Fairy tales, as a motif, allow us to lift the tempo of our writing, cast ourselves against type; write our lives in full dramatic technicolor with queens, princesses, castles, dragons and magic potions. We can rewrite history: this time I get to be the angry giant, the wicked queen; this time, instead of being the princess, we can cast ourselves as the handsome prince and see what life is like from his side of the fence. We can have dialogues between the various protagonists. We can change the ending, have everything turn out differently. Maybe in our story the shoes fits one of the ugly sisters or maybe the carriage gets a puncture and the prince never arrives.

Fairy tales allow us to take a very familiar structure with very familiar archetypes and then write part of our own story, project it onto a much larger stage using that structure. It can allow us to tackle painful issues, see new perspectives on how things are, change the ending and see how we feel about that.

Writing through fairy tales also frees us up in a way that can really help. Sometimes we can feel stuck not only in our lives but in our writing. Rereading your journal entries, you might perhaps be struck by how whiny you sound: woe is me; life didn't turn out quite as I expected. Maybe you cast yourself too often as the victim of circumstances. Writing in the fairy tale genre can produce unexpected results. Maybe you can see yourself adopting different roles. You can have fun, exploring other sides to your story. Instead of being the victim of the piece, you can take the role of the evil stepmother, the wicked queen. Try it. See where it takes you.

In the following sequence of exercises you get to use the same motif but the exercises prompt you to explore your own life using that structure. You can write it simply or you can write it with more complexity. Maybe you'd like to see what life was like from the viewpoint of the wicked stepmother in Snow White. After all, she'd had it good. She was for years and years the fairest in all the land. Maybe it wasn't any picnic for her that she was losing her looks. Maybe, after all, the story of Snow White isn't just about jealousy and what it can do but about sadness, about aging, about loss.

Maybe it's no picnic for the ugly sisters in Cinderella either. All they wanted was a happy ending for themselves. Nobody ever arrived at their door to give them a dig out with magical carriages and horses. They had to graft for every invitation and try to look as presentable as possible. Maybe it's a story of things not turning out well, of always being second best.

In the fairy story structure you can simply dive in, explore where it takes you. In the following exercises you get a chance to play against type, to have fun with your own story. You may wonder: what's the point? What's all this childhood stuff got to do with you? The answer is everything because in writing, using this structure, you are still writing your own story. You are using this structure to explore fresh aspects, writing it slant.

Exercise One: *Once Upon a Time...*

Simply write a story, any story beginning with the words Once Upon a Time...
See where it takes you.

Then maybe write the story again another time and alter the roles.

Or write the whole story from the point of view of a minor character (for example, how did Red Riding Hood's granny feel about what happened?)

Write from the point of view of whichever dwarf you feel like today: Grumpy? Sleepy? Happy? Depending on whose viewpoint you take, you might see a different ending to the story.

Exercise Two: *The Footlights Beckon*

All the world's a stage,
And all the men and women merely players;
They have their exits and their entrances,
And one man in his time plays many parts,
His acts being seven ages.

Shakespeare, *As You Like It*

In our lives we play many parts.
What was the best part you ever got to play?
What was the worst?
What role do you still dream about playing? Write the main character of this role and maybe a speech they might give.
Did you ever audition for a role and not get it? (Job/relationship)
Have you ever made a dramatic entrance or exit?
What kind of roles do you like? High drama? Comedy? Farce? Romance?

Exercise Three: *The Big Adventure*

Begin the story again with the words Once Upon a Time...
In this story take yourself on a journey. Go to faraway lands, maybe on a magic carpet, maybe on a ship. Have a big adventure. Seek the treasure whatever that may be. Do you find it? What happens? How do you get there? Does your ship get blown off course? Where do you end up? How do you survive? Do you get home again? If so what's changed? How have you changed?

Exercise Four: *When You Get to Become the Big, Bad Wolf*

Take a stock character from any story you like and write in the first person from that character's viewpoint.

You could write as the wolf that blew the little pigs houses down. Maybe you were lonely and looking for company. Maybe actually all you wanted to do was to have a bit of fun and the whole thing went horribly wrong. You hadn't meant to destroy anything.

You could write from the point of view of the princess who fell asleep for a hundred years. Maybe you feel terribly guilty about everyone you knew, having to sleep for that long. Or maybe you didn't want any prince to come and rescue you. Maybe all you ever wanted was a bit of peace and quiet and all these fairy godmothers and princes were just interfering in your life.

Exercise Five: *The Whole of the Moon*

In the memorable lyrics of the Waterboys song the hero gets to see the whole of the moon.

People who are visionary can have a profound effect on our lives. We can't help but admire their courage to stand back from the day-to-day humdrum and look at the world in a different way. Recently I watched an episode of *Grand Designs*, the programme presented by Kevin Mc Cloud on unusual house projects. In this programme he revisited an innovative social housing project near Brighton. In 1998, a young father of one who was then living in a caravan, touring around and working casually as a potato picker, decided to try to get a house he could afford for his family. He started a social housing scheme with the help of the local council and recruited interested others. Each family agreed to give thirty hours free labour each week to build the houses for themselves and the other families in the co-op. Though none of the group had ever worked in the building trade they managed to build the beautifully designed wooden houses slowly over the course of the next two years. What Kevin Mc Cloud found when he revisited ten years later was astonishing. Every one of the families was still there. The children, now in their late teens, had bonded closely as a group, as had their parents and because the families weren't paying high rents, they had been able to develop their careers, go back to college. All of the adults interviewed acknowledged that their lives had changed profoundly and it had all begun with one man's idea to build himself an affordable house.

Now try writing about someone you know that sees life like this: who is not afraid to see the bigger picture, who dares to think outside the box, who dares to dream big: someone who sees the whole of the moon.

Exercise Six: The Treasure

Imagine that you are the keeper of the treasure. Describe what that is like. You might describe the treasure itself. What is it like to mind this treasure every day? What does it mean to you?

Exercise Seven: Your Castle

In the 1940s novel, *I Capture the Castle*, Dodie Smith tells the story of family life in a decaying castle told through the journal of a teenager. The castle itself is like a central character in the book.

Describe your own fantasy castle. You can have turrets, moats – anything you like really. The sky is the limit. Now describe your favourite room there. What is the view like? Is it sunny there? What sounds can you hear? What furniture is there? Is there a cupboard? Open it and see what's inside. Is there a table? Does it have a drawer? Open it and see what it holds.

Exercise Seven: You Rule the World

Imagine that you've just taken over as king (or queen) of all the land. Write an open letter to all your subjects introducing yourself, your plans and hopes for the future and telling them the way things are going to be around here from now on.

Having explored the world of fantasy, we come now right back down to the world of everyday objects, which can be very revealing when it comes to writing about our lives.

11

Writing From the Everyday

Everyday objects can foster wonderful writing because these often humble objects are the silent witnesses to our lives. This chapter is about how you can use objects like a button box, an empty box, photographs and fabrics to stimulate memory and writing.

Through reading the books of Gillie Bolton and other writing facilitators, I began, early on in my work as a facilitator, to use all kinds of objects in working with groups: a box of buttons evokes all sorts of memories from times when... Maybe because learning to button things is something we all have to do, when we hold a duffel coat button or a plain white button like you might find on a school shirt, strong memories of our childhood are evoked; times too with our own children when they were little. Silk covered buttons bring you back to that dress you had with the wonderful blue buttons.

Exercise One: The Button Box

The idea for this exercise came from the work of Gillie Bolton who has used the button box for many years. When you think about it, buttoning and unbuttoning are everyday activities, ones we do completely on automatic pilot. You may well have a box of buttons which you can use to rifle through.

If you have, then why not throw them all out on the table and, without thinking too much about it, pick one up and begin to write. Use your senses. How does the button feel? Smooth and polished? Or is it a grainy wooden one? What colour is it? Sometimes it's the most ordinary buttons, the plain little white buttons that are used on men's shirts, the standard blue buttons from school uniform shirts, these are the buttons with which we may be most familiar. You take it in your hand and you may find yourself immediately transported back to a particular time and place when you wore that school shirt every day.

Here is an example of what one writer remembered.

Wooden Buttons

Cold, winter mornings going to school smelt of damp wool and felt rough to the touch. We all had duffle coats; wooden buttons, large for small fingers, were pushed through brown leather loops. There was a musty, close smell in the cloakroom. With five children and a tiny kitchen, there was little room for hanging wet coats to dry after the long walk home. The coats were dark and dull; I don't remember any colours but brown or black; girls and boys wore the same. Maybe they had been navy or green once, but after several hand-me-downs, were now blended, indescribable shades of our collective lives.

We didn't care about clothes then or what we looked like. Well, that's not quite true! When my Mom and Nana dragged me sulking through a 'nice' shop to try on dresses for my 7th birthday, I hated the 'lovely' white-patterned dress with brown trim. Brown trim! Even my tomboy self knew that was strange for a girl. I remember pouting outside the dressing room as negotiations, long-forgotten now, took place diplomatically and sensitively at first, but then the dress with the brown trim and buttons was bought. I also remember being directed to my room before the birthday party to put it on and stop complaining. Staring in the mirror, I wondered what possible appeal this garment held for my mother!

My school uniform had only two large, burgundy buttons at the waist of the gymslip. Gym? It was a vile, heavy, gabardine material which would have kept a docker warm in sub-zero temperatures and we baked in its sackcloth. It made our legs itch as it stung our skin like nettles in early summer heat. The nuns insisted on white nylon gloves in summer and black or brown gloves in winter. Black or brown. Institutional colours of childhood, teamed with mustard or green hand-knitted sweaters. Thank God, these trappings were nuisances for the few seconds in which we put them on. Our lives were coloured by the fields, flowers, animals, birds, rivers, lakes and the freedom to roam for miles on our adventures. Strange locals, like Mrs Carson who minded the huge reservoir, even with one leg shorter than the other, and characters we adored, like the blacksmith, filled our lives and imaginations with smooth, flowing colour.

Marion Cox 🐚

Now, holding a button you have chosen in your hand, begin to write about A Time When...

Exercise Two: *Sweets*

I recently stopped to buy milk in a small newsagents in Galway, tucked away at the end of a housing estate. But there on the counter among the sweets I spied a Macaroon bar. I hadn't seen a Macaroon bar in many years. It was my bar of choice when I was trudging the mile and a half to and from national school at five years old. My sister and myself would stop at Mr Mc Carthy's shop half way on our journey and I would buy a Macaroon bar.

Of course, when I saw the bar that day in the newsagents, I bought it and, with my first bite, I savoured again the soft crunchy chocolate which transported me back to that time and place.

It's all the everyday objects of our lives which accompany us through many of our happiest and saddest times. It's interesting to hear nostalgic conversations between adults on the sweets of their childhood. Grown men and women can recall so vividly the specific smell and taste of sherbets and Bulls Eyes.

You could try this exercise: buy a sweet or bar of chocolate you remember from childhood. Taste it, smell it. Now write about A Time When...

Exercise Three: My *Favourite Dress/Coat/Jumper*

You don't always have to have the object itself to start writing. While I use fabrics sometimes in groups to stimulate memories or other writing, you could also just spend time thinking about your all time favourite dress or coat or hat.

We all have experiences involving clothes which we can vividly recall. To this day I can summon up the memory of standing in the changing room of Topshop in Oxford Street, twirling around in front of the mirror as Elton John and Kiki Dee blasted from the stereo: 'Don't go breaking my heart. I won't go breaking your heart.' I wore those mint green bell-bottom trousers with pride at discos during the following college year.

The defiant and brave choices we made as teenagers to wear that impossibly short red dress stay with us, those wonderful jeans no one else had, the terrible sense of embarrassment at wearing the wrong thing. Debs dresses, wedding suits and dresses, baby clothes – all of these memories can be mined. Ernest Hemingway wrote what is possibly the most poignant six word short story about a pair of baby shoes:

> For sale: baby shoes; never worn.

Write about your most vivid memory of clothes you wore, the clothes you adored and the ones you hated with a passion.

Exercise Four: *Surprised by Joy*

'Surprised by Joy' is the title of one of Wordsworth's sonnets describing a moment of joy which he longed to share. It can happen just when you're not expecting it.

Recently I met someone at the swimming pool who told me about an event that had happened the previous evening at Blackrock in Salthill, Galway. It's a place where people swim all year round. She was just coming out of the water. It was high tide on a stormy evening in late September. The water was so choppy that the spray doused the swimmers even before they were in the water. As my friend got out, a German tourist, a woman, looked on and said, 'I envy you.' Without hesitation, my friend suggested that she take her towel and swim suit and go in herself. So the tourist did. The other swimmers, mainly men, stayed in the water to offer her help in case she needed it in the heavy swell of the sea. Ten minutes later she emerged, glowing and laughing to say, 'For the rest of my life I'm going to make sure I keep on coming back here for more of that.'

The words 'Surprised by Joy' came to mind when I heard that story. Sometimes, especially when you're not looking for it, when you happen to have gone for an evening stroll from your hotel along the seafront you might find yourself surprised by joy, submerged in the waves you thought would be too cold, too rough, surrounded by a bunch of people who have suddenly become friends.

So have you ever been surprised by joy?
Write about that moment.
Who else was there?
What happened then?

Exercise Five: Gifts

The exchange of gifts between friends and family is a regular source of joy and happiness, though sometimes fraught with anxiety too: what to give; how much to spend; or even whether to give at all.

Write about a gift you would like to receive (it might be the gift of some free time, a little attention, a chance to shine).

OR

Write about a gift you would like to give. Who is the lucky recipient? How do you think they might react?

Exercise Six: The Empty Box

Imagine a beautiful white empty box in front of you on a table. It has a lovely carved cover and smooth white sides. Inside is empty with a soft red velvet lining. This is a memory box for safekeeping of all memories. You have the opportunity now to put one memory in the box. Write about what you would like to put in the box for safekeeping.

I hope in this chapter you managed to mine some memories of objects past and present.

Now we come to looking at the four seasons, of times of special significance in each year. The cyclical nature of events like Christmas often evoke strong memories good and bad. We explore different times of the year and their significance to us.

12

Writing Through the Seasons

The seasons form the natural rhythm by which we live. Our distant memories of seasons long ago may be a bit rose tinted, especially now with all the talk of global warming. Were the summers really long and hot? Did it not rain as much as it does now?

Regardless of the weather, we often remember events by the season in which they happened: that was the summer I got my first job; we went to Paris in the spring and it really was beautiful and that was when I knew I was in love; that autumn we swept the leaves on the path for the last time. Or we associate seasons with particular feelings: cosy winter fires; endless summer days; spring cleaning.

Maybe you have a favourite season, maybe you don't but the chances are that these exercises will trigger memories of specific times in your life which you associate with a particular time of year.

Exercise One: *The Rainy Season*

> It is the rainy season that gives wealth.
>
> *African Saying*

Living in what is often a rain-sodden country, I can testify that you either have to see the merits of the rain or else just moan about it the way a lot of people do. It is tough when it rains incessantly, especially during the summer or when a big outdoor event is planned, but rain gives Ireland a very fertile soil, making it a great agricultural country. There are some benefits like the saying above states.

What have been the benefits for you during what might be called the rainy periods of your life when the sun didn't shine every day? Sometimes going through a bleak time can make us more resourceful, more self-reliant.
What was your rainy season?
What wealth did it bring?

Exercise Two: *The Store Cupboard*

The autumn is a time for storing things up: presents, food/drink for Christmas; wood/turf/coal for winter fires. We squirrel away, looking forward to the time of celebration to come.

We do the same thing in our lives. Somehow through all the crises and disasters that may happen from time to time, the things we didn't see coming, somehow we manage to store up some good things along the way.

What are the good things that you have stored up over the course of your life?
What are the things you hold in your heart?
It could be:
A friendship, maybe one that dates back years.
A relationship that has been carefully steered through troubled waters.

In the song 'The Voyage', Christy Moore writes:

> Life is an ocean and love is a boat
> In troubled water that keeps us afloat.

So write about your own relationship, your marriage, your long-term partner. What is it that this relationship has meant to you?

OR

Write about a wonderful memory to which you often return.
Write about the store cupboard of your heart. Take a look around. What's in there?

Exercise Three: *Accountancy Review*

We often say: where does all the time go? This year, take stock in the same way that old Scrooge is forced to do in *A Christmas Carol*. Stop and do an old-fashioned accountancy review of your year, as if you were entering all this information in one of those big ledger books.

What were the goods/services received during this year from other people? What things were you given that made a significant difference to your life? What were your outgoings/expenditures: what did you invest a lot of energy in? What did you give to other people?
What does the grand total look like? Do the books balance? Have you received as much or more than you feel you gave?
Now try writing your goals for next year in terms of expenditures and incomings: what will you invest your time and energy in? What do you hope to receive back into your life?

Exercise Four: *My Favourite Time of the Year*

When I worked in Dublin, I travelled on a dual carriageway into work every day. In springtime, the central reservation that divided the road was always planted with daffodils which bloomed for a few weeks every spring. No matter what kind of mood I might be in, the sight of all those flowers dancing in the wind always lifted my heart.

What is the season that lifts your heart every year? What are the sights, the smells, the sounds?

Here is one writer's take on the winter and all that it brings.

❧ *Winter's fingers*

Whipping winds and driving rain,
The season's certain change again,
The roaring surf and searching seas,
Scattered leaves and naked trees.

All pass me by as I ignore,
The furious strength and deafening roar,
From where I lie in quiet rest,
Sharp weather's edges make no ingress.

I see my friends they come and go,
and faithful visitors I'll never know.
Flowers and candles embrace this place
As gentle touches on my face.

Summer distant long forgotten
The pastel shades of Autumn gone
the flowers and petals in mulches rotting
As Winter's early tendrils spawn.

Iain Mac Clean ❧

Exercise Five: The Winter of Our Discontent

Now is the winter of our discontent
Made glorious summer by this sun of York

Shakespeare's *Richard III*

The opening lines of the play *Richard III* declare that the long winter of discontent is over now that Richard has taken his place on the throne beckoning in a glorious summer.

Write about your own winter of discontent. It could have been a time when you didn't have a job or you were lonely in a new place or you had just broken up with someone.
So how did the discontent end?
Was it followed by a glorious summer?

Exercise Six: Cabin Fever

Deep in the heart of winter when the weather is cold, with seemingly endless rain or even snow and the darkness falls in late afternoon, we can feel like we have cabin fever, hemmed in by the weather and the lack of light. It echoes a feeling we may have had at other times in our life; a feeling of being stuck with no real means of escape. For example, being at home all day every day with small children or being stuck in a low-paid job with no future plans of getting out of it, feeling trapped in a relationship.

Write about a time when you experienced cabin fever, feeling stuck.
How did you escape?
How did you dig yourself out?
What happened then?

Exercise Seven: A Memorable Christmas

And then there is Christmas. We all probably have vivid memories of Christmas at some stage in our lives. Usually people have strong feelings one way or the other about the whole festive season. Christmas is likely to evoke feelings of nostalgia for some who adore the sense of tradition and spend a lot of time in preparation for the day itself. In these recessionary times, it can often mean either a lonely time because family members are far away or joy at their arrival home. Others feel that the whole thing is an overrated time of expense and hype.

Here's one writer's memory of the worst Christmas ever for her in the late 1960s. Though the story is set almost forty years ago, there are so many people working away during these times, it probably has just as much significance today.

❧ Worst Ever Christmas

Time: 1967

Place: Birmingham, UK.

News: Headlines: Foot and Mouth spreading rapidly.

The Effect: Irish government appeals to all Irish citizens:

DON'T COME HOME FOR CHRISTMAS

We were told we could carry this infection into Ireland, and, of course, our economy was very dependent on farming and its subsidiary industries, milk and its by products: cheese, cream, meats and by products, e.g. sausage, pudding. It was clear that if the dreaded Foot and Mouth entered our country, it would be disastrous to the animals, and devastating for our economy.

Result: My sister Kay and I complied with the request.

Home: We shared a one-roomed bedsitter, large, but cramped. It was furnished with twin beds, a wardrobe, dressing table, basic cooking facilities, a table and two chairs, wash-up facilities, storage for pots, pans, and dishes and utensils. A gas fire provided heating, when one popped coins into the slot meter. But this also caused much condensation. Combined with the cooking smells, this was very bad for Kay. She has suffered always from severe asthma.

This is where we cooked, ate, washed up, slept, studied, and ironed our clothes after a visit to the launderette. In this one room, we lived our lives after work. We made the most of it. Kay took a walk most evenings, to give me quietness to study. Such were the conditions in the 1960s, and we were by no means the only ones living thus. And this is where we spent our Christmas, in the year 1967.

About a mile from our 'home' lived our Uncle Frank, our Dad's youngest brother. His wife Carmel and son Dermot lived in a nice house. We kept in touch on a semi-regular basis. As Dad's brother, I think he had promised him to keep an eye out for us. But, the hoped for invitation to Christmas dinner did not materialise. We were asked to tea, later on Christmas Day.

After morning Mass at the nearest church, back we went to our lonely home. I've no doubt we had decorated it a little, with a crib, some colourful decorations, perhaps candles, to create a homely and cheerful atmosphere. What we cooked for our Christmas dinner I cannot remember. But we made an effort not to be miserable, so far from family, friends, and neighbours. We had a transistor radio, a great treat in that era. No doubt we listened to it during part of the long lonely day. We also read a lot, always. Perhaps we continued to knit, as we often made pullovers and jumpers for our younger siblings in Tuam. Our Mum had taught us to knit from an early age; we still enjoy that craft.

We were probably twenty and twenty-two years then. As my birthday is just three days before Christmas, that had also been a lonely day for me. Kay had to work. Bordsley College had closed for the seasonal holidays, and so I was alone until Kay returned from work after six o'clock.

After dark we huddled into our warmest coats, scarves, hats and boots. We took a brisk walk to Uncle

Frank's house. It was quite a pleasant evening there. Of course we had a really nice tea, with the turkey and trimmings we had no means of cooking for ourselves in our tiny oven with two rings on top. Most people then did not even dream of owning a car. Uncle was no exception. Later we walked home, but I cannot remember if Uncle Frank accompanied us. I think not. It was quite safe to walk the streets way back then.

As with cars, telephones were for the rich and wealthy. There was no opportunity to talk to and hear the voices of our parents and siblings. Our loved ones were far away, and we could 'see' what was happening in our family home, from years of living Christmas there, with our loved ones. So many were there, gathered around the TV, sharing stories, admiring new toys, books, board games, lots of laughter, fun, and joy, twinkling lights on the Christmas tree.

Other older siblings had returned home from college, we alone were apart. It was a surreal day and season. We both knew, but did not voice it, that never would we be away from family again at this holy and blessed season of goodwill. Hindsight is a wonderful teacher. At some point we realised that because we lived in the city, never went into the countryside, we could have gone home for Christmas. As we lived in a town in Ireland, once more we would not be near vulnerable farm animals.

Our government then, as now, caused so much unnecessary upset and loneliness to many families in Ireland, and their loved members resident in the UK. Since that time nearly forty years ago, I have always been with family for Christmas, and Kay and I always talk on the telephone on Christmas Day. We have never talked about this time, our worst Christmas ever.

Cepta Casserly

Now write about a Christmas you'll never forget.

What happened?

Who was there?

Write using all your senses. This should be easy given that we all have pretty vivid sense memories of the sounds of choirs, bells, cooking smells and the vivid reds and greens of Christmas holly.

In the next chapter, we focus on our own sense of ourselves; the narrative of our life, how it all hangs together including our hopes and dreams for the future.

13

A Sense of Self

You could say that all of therapeutic writing is about our sense of ourselves. But in fact we are often blind to the self that goes about its business every day. We use phrases like 'I don't know how I ended up here' or 'I can't explain it even to myself'.

We can get so caught up in living that we are not self-aware. In difficult times like a deep recession, we feel that we must just keep our nose to the grindstone and hope that things might just change of their own accord or we don't listen to our gut feelings about things. We ignore our inner-self and what it is saying.

This chapter gives you an opportunity to try some exercises that just focus on your sense of yourself in a direct way.

Exercise One: Beginning Something New

Until one is committed, there is hesitancy, the chance to draw back – Concerning all acts of initiative (and creation), there is one elementary truth that ignorance of which kills countless ideas and splendid plans: that the moment one definitely commits oneself, then Providence moves too. All sorts of things occur to help one that would never otherwise have occurred. A whole stream of events issues from the decision, raising in one's favour all manner of unforeseen incidents and meetings and material assistance, which no one could have dreamed would have come his way. Whatever you can do, or dream you can do, begin it. Boldness has genius, power, and magic in it. Begin it now.

Goethe

There are times in our lives when we reach some sort of tipping point. We have talked maybe for a long time about doing something: maybe it's about taking time off to travel, maybe it's about having children or writing the great novel. It could be something like a decision to get fit or lose weight or get a dog or take up football again.

We may have got to the brink more than once where we almost did it; we almost went for it. However, as the quotation above says, there is always the chance to 'draw back' and, as one of life's eternal ditherers myself, I feel a huge sense of solidarity for the ditherers who can't just do it. It's actually interesting to see the current popularity of the slogan 'Just do it' on t-shirts. A lot of people are walking around declaring their intention to get on with it.

This exercise is all about the doing of 'it' whatever 'it' is. I also happen to think Goethe is right on how, once you begin, all sorts of things seem to come into play, to conspire to help you on your way. Maybe this is because your attention is now on the goal and that focus makes you sit up and notice things you filtered out before.

If, like me, you have a big wish to take the Trans Siberian Express then you might just find that once you go and buy the tickets, you start seeing articles about Mongolia, you happen to bump into someone whose sister just did the trip and on and on. Serendipity? Maybe or maybe like Goethe says, commitment changes everything.

Mary Oliver, the poet, exhorts us to seize the day by asking, 'Tell me, what is it that you plan to do with your one wild and precious life?'

So try this exercise:
What is it that you will do with your one wild and precious life?
What is it that you want to begin?
What is it that is stopping you?

Exercise Two: *When Everything Changed*

Tectonics is the study of the earth's plates. When the plates shift there may be enormous consequences for the inhabitants of the planet: earthquakes, tsunamis. Everything changes.

Recall a moment when you realised that nothing would ever be the same again. Or maybe you could not realise anything then but you see now that something shifted in your sense of who you were at a certain moment in your past. Perhaps at the time you were paralysed, numb. Now you can stand outside that moment. Now you can speak for yourself.

What do you see? If you can, describe the setting. Where were you? What is under your feet? What is above you? Who is there? What is the light like?

As you describe this moment, as you place it (recall its setting) tell how you felt.

What were you doing? What were others in the scene doing?

Can you recall what anyone said?

Exercise Three: *How You Have Changed*

This exercise is about reviewing how we see ourselves; how circumstances have changed us. Often after a serious illness, a near-death experience, people talk about how they have changed; how they now realise what is important. Maybe you have been pulled up short by an event in your life. It could have been losing your job, a divorce or it could have been a wonderful happening like falling in love or having your first child.

Now without thinking about it too much, complete the following sentence a few times.

> I used to be ... but now I'm ...
>
> I used to be ... but now I'm ...
>
> I used to be ... but now I'm ...

Continue with one of these sentences.

OR try one of the following:

Write in the voice of the before self, then write in the voice of the now self. The before self could be a childhood voice or a teenage voice or you as a young adult. It could be from any period of your life. Write about what has changed.

OR

Try writing as if you are the interviewer and the interviewee about some major event in your life, inventing the questions and answers. Write the dialogue between yourself and the imagined interviewer looking at this event as objectively as you can.

Questions that are often asked in this kind of interview are:

What have you learned?

What would you do differently?

Any regrets?

If you could go back, what is the one thing you would change?

What words of advice would you give to your younger self?

Exercise Four: *The Milestones of Our Lives*

The milestones we actually see as important are often not the usual ones like going to college, first job, getting married, leaving home, emigrating. It's often different sorts of milestones that strike us as especially significant: a time when we suddenly realised something for the first time: 'What am I doing living with these people, I need to get my own place.' Or we decided something for ourselves, came to a momentous decision about leaving someone or going back to someone or telling someone a long-held secret.

Now write a list of milestones in your life.

Then complete these sentences:

The day I realised...

The day I decided...

The day I found out...

Now pick one to continue writing.

Exercise Five: *Between Two Places/Two Worlds*

At the end of *A World of Winnie the Pooh*, Christopher Robin stands on the cusp of his new life in boarding school as a small child. He has to say goodbye to his old world of 'doing nothing'. In his poignant conversation with Pooh, he tries to work out what it will all mean and, more importantly, how to say goodbye to his old world of enchantment. It was always a source of great glee for my children when they were small that I never managed to get through that story at bedtime without my voice faltering and my eyes filling up. It describes a process we have all experienced at some point of how hard it can be to let go of what we hold dear and move on to unknown and scary new pastures.

Have you ever stood between two separate worlds and had to choose? What was that like?

Have two separate worlds ever collided? Like when your whole family comes to visit you in the new place you live and meet all your new friends? What was that like?

What do you miss about the worlds to which you have said goodbye? Your home town? Your childhood friends? A country you used to live in? Your college friends you don't see now?

Exercise Six: *Doubt and Certainty*

The whole problem with the world is that fools and fanatics are always so certain of themselves, and wiser people so full of doubts.

Bertrand Russell

Describe a time in your life when you were foolishly certain (yes, I just know he's the one...) or a time when you were wisely full of doubts (hang on a second here...).

Exercise Seven: *Your Own Discovery*

We are too ready, perhaps, to wed ourselves to visions which keep us safe from personal discovery.

Miller Mair
(Addressing the Psychotherapy Section
of the British Psychological Society, 1988)

In our world of mass communication we are exposed to dogma all the time: we are told how to live, how to be with each other, how to have sex, how to raise our children, even how to die. As a result, we often feel guilty that somehow we're missing the point, not getting it right. But it's good sometimes to think completely for yourself; not what your best friend says, your partner. Just you.

Write down something that you feel is your own personal discovery. What is it that you have come to truly know?

Exercise Eight: *A Sense of Identity*

In the great novel *Stoner* by John Williams, the main protagonist lies alone and dying at the end of his life. To others, his life has not been particularly special in any way. After a mediocre academic career and a difficult marriage, he will quickly be forgotten. But in the midst of everything not working out that well, Stoner acted authentically. So at the end of his life and alone, he sees this clearly for himself. 'A sense of his own identity came upon him with a sudden force, and he felt the power of it. He was himself and he knew what he had been.'

What is it that you have been?
What is your own sense of yourself? Not what others say you are; what do you think you are, have been? What is it that you are all about? What drives you? What defines you?

And now onwards to the world of work which throws up endless opportunities to write, including writing about your dreams and future plans!

14

Writing and Work

There was a scene on an old political satire programme on Irish television many moons ago. A canny politician was giving a pre-election speech outside a church on Sunday. A crowd had gathered and were listening attentively to his every word. For every promise he made there were cheers. Finally he shouted: 'And I'll make sure you all get work.' There were murmurs throughout the crowd but no cheers. He repeated the promise with even greater gusto but again no cheers. Someone whispered in his ear and then he shouted: 'I'll make sure you all get jobs.' The crowd cheered loudly.

This chapter is all about work but not necessarily about jobs. The two are often equated in our heads. When someone asks what do you do, they generally mean what do you earn a living at, what is your job. We define ourselves so much by the jobs we hold. But sometimes not having a job to define you can make all the difference to the eventual outcome.

In an interview in the *New Yorker* magazine in July 2012, Bruce Springsteen and his lifelong friend and fellow member of the E Street Band, Steve Van Zandt, reflected on how they came to become one of the most successful rock bands ever. The interview catalogues the early days of the band in New Jersey, working casual jobs and saving food stamps while camping out in a surfboard factory run by their manager. Steve van Zandt recalls: 'Remember, we didn't go into this life because we were courageous or brilliant. We were the last guys standing. Anyone with a choice to do something else – be a dentist, get a real job, *whatever* – took it!'

At this moment you may have a job you love or a job that bores you. You may have recently retired and are missing work colleagues. You may have a job that you find difficult and stressful. You may not know yet what you want to do or you may be unemployed and looking for some kind of work.

In this chapter the exercises explore a wider aspect than the job you may or may not have at this moment. Instead we will look at your passions, what you like to do; your skills, the things you do well. We will also look at ways you can write reflectively about your work, as in the job you do.

Exercise One: *You Before/You Now*

As part of Turku, Finland's 2011 European Capital of Culture events, Candy Chang, an artist, was commissioned to create a public art project near the University of Turku. She decided to turn a popular pedestrian/bike path between the halls of residence and the university into an interactive space with fill-in-the-blank sentences stencilled on the pavement that said 'When I was little I wanted to be ... Today I want to be ...'

The aim was to compare yourself today and when you were young, reflecting on how you've changed or stayed the same. Passersby used chalk to write directly on the pavement. These are some of the responses recorded in the artist's web page:

- When I was little I wanted to be a bird. Today I want to be a speech therapist.
- When I was little I wanted to be a grown up. Today I want to be a kid.
- When I was little I wanted to be a princess. Today I want to be an electrician.
- When I was little I wanted to be a teacher. Today I want to be a teacher.

Try this exercise for yourself. Write the sentence out three times or even more filling the blank spaces each time. Repeating a sentence several times often helps us to probe deeper into what it is we really want to say. So,write out the sentence below several times:

When I was little I wanted to be ... today I want to be ...

Then read back your sentences, pick the one you relate to the most and start writing.

Exercise Two: *A Skill I Learned*

Over the course of a lifetime we learn many skills. At national school, I was taught to knit and dressmake. Looking back, of course, you might say how sexist it was that only the girls got to do that but they are skills I'm glad I have even if they are seldom used. Because of those skills, every summer I take the big beach blanket I knitted a few years back (actually a loose knitted jacket) on beach strolls. If a button or hem needs to be fixed, I don't baulk at the task and, as a fourteen-year-old teenager, I solved the problem of a boring summer by making all my own clothes. Any knitter will tell you that knitting is an incredibly soothing thing to do so I am glad that Sr Benedict made us learn to cast on and off, to top stitch, to make darts and even how to make a kilt! Once out of the confines of what Sr Benedict thought we should make, I found knitting and sewing to be very creative.

So describe a skill you have learned.
Who taught you this skill?
What has this skill meant to you?
Have you passed this skill on to anyone else?

Exercise Three: *My First (or Second) Job Ever*

We all have memories of work experiences. Our earliest work experiences often leave indelible memories, maybe because we are all eyes and ears, drinking everything in. It's all so new and strange. Seared into my brain is the look on the matron's face when she opened the washing machine in the Children's Home I worked in (my second summer job) to find that all the white towelling nappies had turned pink, the same colour as the bibs which I had been told but had forgotten, SHOULD BE WASHED SEPARATELY. But I also vividly remember the exquisite taste of the homemade cherry pie we had almost every night at dinner.

Here the writer picked a bar of soap from a group of objects in a group exercise and was reminded of one of her first jobs.

✿ Colonial Candles

Palmolive Original Soap with olive oil, wrapped in smooth, waxed paper. Soothing greens brush the paper around the label, with a pair of olives nesting like birds' eggs in the corner. Broad, white spaces make me think of freshness, water, purity. The paper reminds me of the treasures enclosed in all paper; words, stories, gifts. The soap is soft to touch; my finger slides over its waxed surface. Its scent is strong, singular, flowery, invigorating.

The soap reminds me of Colonial Candles, the factory at the end of Main St, Hyannis, Massachusetts. Jumbled together, Irish students, American college kids, transient grannies living in RVs (recreational vehicles) and locals; we worked happily, noisily, side-by-side on the crude, old-fashioned but simple assembly lines.

The scent of Christmas Holly, Green Ivy, Cranberry Delight, Pumpkin Pie (the large pillar candles), blended with the body odour and cheap perfumes. Bertha, the transient granny, regaled us with her stories of life on the road. She was four-foot-nothing behind the wheel of the enormous RV in the parking lot. Doris put Kleenex up sleeves, down trousers, between collar and neck, and scratched constantly. Her hair was cut short but styled so well that you could picture her dressed in a business suit. She stared vacantly and mumbled, lost from a life before brain surgery.

I was assigned to the perfumed, cosmetic candles; 1 oz of Estee Lauder in a tiny china jar, costing half a week's wages. So, eight and a half hours later, when I sat on the silver bar stool in Dunkin'

Donuts, eating my Apple Cinnamon donut, I smelt like a million dollars and looked like I needed a dime.

Marion Cox

Now try writing a memory from one of your earliest jobs.

What happened?

Who else was there?

How did things turn out?

What, if anything, did you learn?

Exercise Four: *How Do You Doodle?*
Finding the Work You Were Born to Do

> That in the end I may find
> Something not sold for a penny
> In the slums of mind.
>
> Patrick Kavanagh, *Ascetic*

In Patrick Kavanagh's poem 'Ascetic' he describes a long and painful search for something of real meaning. Many of us experience the search for a meaningful job that we love as also being a long and often painful journey.

That longing to find the kind of work that makes us want to jump out of bed in the morning is not helped by a deep recession in which young people are given the message that all the jobs are in this sector or that sector and to train in that field, without any attention getting paid to what it is that ignites their passion. People already in jobs don't dare to leave with the prospect of unemployment rearing its head.

Yet we often daydream about the work we would like to do. All those chef programmes are classic examples of square pegs in round holes. The would-be chefs are invariably in gainful employment like banking or IT and would cheerfully ditch their highly successful, well-paid careers to obtain a place in Chef X's kitchen because 'it's always been my dream to cook'.

I always wanted to write but it wasn't something I spent a whole lot of time doing. There were occasional times when I did immerse myself in it but I also forgot about writing for long periods, times when I did other things like training to be a clinical psychologist. In the end I would always find myself coming back to some old battered notebook and picking up the pen again. I went on to work as a psychologist, then did a management degree and started lecturing and training.

Many years later I read a book by Nick Williams called *The Work We Were Born to Do*. It was eye-opening because instead of trying to figure out something like a logical career, the author instead spoke about finding your passion, the heartbeat of your life, what you kept coming back to.

He asked a question that really stopped me in my tracks and made me think. When no one else was bothering you or asking you to do something else, particularly as a child, what did you do? I was immediately transported back to me aged twelve, doodling in the back of my school notebooks, writing plays, funny scenes. I was a doodler and not a drawing kind of doodler, a writing doodler.

That was it. Here at last was the passion I had been chasing, albeit very intermittently all my life.

Try to remember. What was it you did when you were just hanging around? For today's generation of children, there is probably too much time structuring their activities, arranging play dates. For my generation, there was plenty of downtime. I often spent that time reading or occasionally writing.

What did you do in the downtime? Were you always to be found tinkering with some old machine or gadget, wondering how all the parts were put together? Were the back pages of your copies at school filled with dresses you had designed? Sometimes in our lives we feel a deep yearning for something which underpins everything. It could be that the clues are already there. Think about what you tend to do even now when you have some down time, when no one is asking you to put out the bins or collect the kids.

Now complete these sentences:

> As a child, I really loved to spend my time...
>
> Now I really love to spend my time...

Keep on writing once you've finished these sentences.

Exercise Five: *Reflecting on Your Current Work*

I teach seminars on reflective writing for clinical psychology students, nursing students, those working in primary care and in social care. Teaching people the ability to reflect on their own feelings in relation to their work is an important way for them to get distance from issues that can be challenging and traumatic.

So here is your chance to reflect on your work:
Maybe there is something really bugging you about your work. Maybe there's something you want to change about the 'way we do things around here'. Write an unsent letter to your boss. Now write back in the voice of your boss.

Exercise Six: *Office Metaphors*

Here is a list of metaphors used to describe typical office situations. Pick one that jumps out at you and start to write

- The rumour mill.
- The grapevine.
- Working like Trojans.
- A team player.
- Backstabbing.
- In the firing line.
- At the coalface.
- Up to my tonsils.
- The glass ceiling.
- Climbing the corporate ladder.

Exercise Seven: *Your Future Self*

In that iconic speech given by Steve Jobs at Stanford University he talked about the need to find and work at what you love: 'Your work is going to fill a large part of your life, and the only way to be truly satisfied is to do what you believe is great work. And the only way to do great work is to love what you do. If you haven't found it yet, keep looking. Don't settle. As with all matters of the heart, you'll know when you find it. And, like any great relationship, it just gets better and better as the years roll on. So keep looking until you find it. Don't settle.' (Stanford commencement speech, June 2005)

Now think about your life in the future. Imagine that you didn't 'settle', that in fact, everything has gone as well as it possibly could. You have worked hard and succeeded at accomplishing all of your life goals. Think of this as the realisation of all your life dreams. Now, write about what you imagine. Write about the kinds of things that absorb you. What do you spend your time doing?

Sometimes life deals us a tough blow. The next chapter is about writing about those times when we have been laid low by illness and, more importantly, how we learned to cope.

15

Writing, Illness, and the Wounded Storyteller

We all have different ways of dealing with being sick but having a serious illness does radically interrupt our life story. Arthur W. Frank, Professor of Sociology at the University of Calgary and a cancer sufferer, likens the experience to a shipwreck, blown entirely off course due to storm conditions. Now the map has to be redrawn, the ship repaired and a new course set.

On 8 December 1995 Jean Dominique Bauby suffered a massive stroke at the age of forty-three which left him paralysed from the neck down in a condition called locked-in syndrome. Due to complications with his right eye, he was left with one way of communicating and that was to blink using only his left eyelid. Prior to his stroke he had been editor of *Elle* magazine. While in hospital he dictated a book, *The Diving Bell and the Butterfly*, which explains what it was like to be trapped in his body which he envisioned as being in an old-fashioned diving suit with a brass helmet. Others 'saw' his spirit which was alive and like a butterfly.

The book took ten months to dictate and took approximately two hundred thousand blinks to write with an average word taking two minutes. He died of pneumonia three days after the book was finished. Apart from the fact that the book is a great read, what is most extraordinary about this story is how someone who loved to write (prior to the stroke, Bauby had planned to write a novel) had the will to tell his story, the desire to express what he was thinking, feeling and experiencing. His project of writing the book also made sense of his life, put a structure in place to his days, gave him something to think about, to plan, to work on with someone else, his translator, who sat with him for four hours a day for ten months.

When people become sick for whatever reason, their illness becomes a story. The medical story predominates. The narrative of the illness must be told and retold for everyone whom you meet in hospital and at clinics. The history of this story is recorded in your chart and you may have several different charts all residing in different locations so the nurses have one story, your doctor another (of course, there may be several medical specialities involved all with their own story), the labs may have another chart and so on it goes. As well as the formal medical history, the more informal story of what has happened must be told and retold to friends and family. Arthur Frank writes that on one day he told eight different versions of his story.

Frank has analysed the stories of illness into three underlying narratives. Everyone's illness story is unique and will combine all three narratives 'each perpetually interrupting the other two ... in any illness all three narrative types are told, alternatively and repeatedly.'

Restitution Narrative
The plot of the restitution narrative has the basic storyline: 'Yesterday I was healthy, today I'm sick, tomorrow I'll be healthy again.' This dominates the stories of most people especially those who are recently ill and who do not have a chronic illness. The storyline is filled out with talk of tests, treatments, results, competence of doctors, alternative treatments. Phrases like 'as good as new' are the core of the restitution narrative. The story is all about health. Frank quotes an example of a prospective restitution story of someone about to go into hospital for surgery. When Frank expresses sympathy for his illness, the man looks at him as if unsure what he is talking about and says, 'It's nothing.' So the restitution narrative is the 'You'll be back on your feet in no time' story. Frank notes that most commercials for non-prescription drugs also follow the restitution narrative with the person in misery from cold/flu/headache, unable to take part in normal life, missing out. Then the remedy is suggested often by a helpful spouse or friend. Then the person is shown happily back to his 'old self'.

Chaos

Chaos is the opposite of restitution. Its plot never imagines life getting better. Chaos stories are as anxiety provoking as restitution stories are preferred. Events are told in a random series of happenings with no discernible order to them. Chaos stories are hard to hear, they threaten us. There is no distance from the story, no ability to reflect from afar on the experience. 'In the chaos story troubles go all the way down to the depths.'

In an article in the *New York Magazine*, writer Michael Wolff tells of his experience of watching his mother being kept alive through the valiant attempts of doctors in spite of the fact that it was not what she wanted and she had no quality of life. So, at eighty-four, with progressive dementia she underwent major heart surgery, survived but with devastating effects on her mental and physical state: 'The operation absolutely repaired my mother's heart – "She can live for years" according to the surgeon (whom we were never to see again) – but left us longing for her level of muddle before the valve job. Where before she had been gently sinking, now we were in freefall.'

Quest

Quest stories meet suffering head on. They accept illness and then use it. The illness is the occasion of a journey that becomes a quest. Something is to be gained from the experience. In quest stories, the interruption of the illness is seen as a challenge which the person must face. The ill person is the teller of her own story and most published accounts of illness are of this type. In a book cited in the resource list at the back of this book, Julie Davey, a Professor of Writing, describes a visit to her oncologist's office. It occurred days after 9/11 when she was in the final stages of recovery from treatment for breast cancer. Out of the window of the office she saw a line of children, cancer patients, led by a volunteer. They were singing. Davey describes the effect on herself, particularly of seeing the volunteer. 'At that defining moment I vowed to do something to try to make a continuing and significant difference in peoples' lives ... I was determined to give something back.' She went on to set up a writing group and eventually wrote a book about the group.

Exercise One: *The Narrative of Illness*

If you or someone close to you has been through an illness, which of the three narratives above makes most sense to you in terms of how you now recall that event?

Restitution (I was sick but am now back to my old self)?
Chaos (it was a huge and terrible muddle)?
Quest (it was very difficult but it changed me/I'm a different person today because of it)?

Now tell the story of that illness.

Exercise Two: *Writing a Letter*

If you have experienced an illness/a problem with a specific part of your body, write to that part now and have that part write a letter back to you (your right shoulder/your knee with arthritis/your weakened eyesight). Here is one such letter written to a breast tumour.

❧ *Dear Tumour*

Dear Tumour,
It is only for the sake of convention and syntax that I'm addressing you as dear ... because you are definitely not held in esteem by me or wanted as part of my life. You sneaked in to my body when I wasn't looking, like a thief in the night. Was it my complacency that you preyed on? Had I relaxed my guard and, sneaky as you are, you had seized the opportunity.

I have no room for any tumour in my body. Any excess weight I have studiously tried to shed by watching my diet and going for walks and cycles. I refused to be tempted by your friends, the cigarettes, didn't associate too much with the giddy and unreliable alcoholic drinks that you hang around with. (I confess I did enjoy the more sophisticated glass of wine occasionally.) So why did you pick my body?

You wormed your way into my breast near my heart, which belonged to me and those I hold dear. Are you surprised therefore that I was merciless when it came to extracting you from my being? I have no regrets that you were stopped in your tracks by some toxic drugs which zapped you and reduced you to a shadow of your former self. Of course, I was also caught in the crossfire. You caused me much pain and grief. My taste buds disappeared with my hair. Everything had a tang of metal in my mouth.

Exhilarated when you were finally yanked out, and exposed on the pathologist's Petri dish and you were prodded and dissected by instruments designed to uncover your secrets. You wonder why I am angry with you after all the indignities that you caused me to encounter. I had never planned to have needles shoved into all parts of my anatomy, or to have wounds which drained into tubes for weeks or to have to learn to raise my arm again and relieve the persistent itch on the top of my shoulder.

However, I am wiser now. I am on my guard. Even though you may be lurking out there somewhere I have taken the advice and made my body very secure. All the latest gadgets I have installed. I know you are repelled by fruits and vegetables, the more colourful the better. The Manuka honey and flax seeds that I sprinkle on my porridge are like a sprinkling of holy water on the evil spirits. The Reiki and reflexology that I practice leaves you a quivering mess. Not to mention the knights in shiny armour that circles me on horseback, Sir Galahad Keane and his team of merry men.

So you are not welcome near me again. I would advise you to give up and perhaps retrain for something that you are good at. Good riddance!

Not Yours Ever either Sincerely or Respectfully,

Breeda O'Connor

Exercise Three: A Time When...

Write about A Time When... in relation to your illness/experiences with hospitals/doctors. It could be the time you got a difficult diagnosis, a time when you felt angry or ignored, or a time when someone went out of their way to be kind and attentive when you needed it.

In the following piece, the writer describes coping with a side effect he did not see coming!

The Last Two Days

Last evening I went round to the River Inn for my *one* pint of Guinness (good for you?). My arrival at the pub which was achieved quickly as the ten minute walk can be tricky in terms of my waning bladder control. However as one door closes another opens and I was delighted to find that I had indeed acquired another bodily weakness to keep me amused! I now enjoy the ability to let go thunderous farts at will!

Wow! I had noticed in the cancer patients handbook that this is a recognised side effect, clearly anatomically incorrect, thank God as I would be liable to blow the lining of my side pocket to kingdom come. Anyway let's forget about the boring anatomy and look at the potential of my new found skill, I hasten not to be taken lightly. My discovery was realised on the very threshold of the door of the River Inn and, as I entered, a gent left (forewarned perhaps). He took the loud report to be an old door clearly in need of lubrication, perhaps not a million miles from the truth!

I entered somewhat sheepishly as a carbon copy of the door noise echoed round the vestibule. I was mortified and embarrassed but the undoubted prize winner of a fart was, to my joy, lost in the cheer of the drinkers as Ireland scored a goal and the TV on the wall was at full blast – that made two of us. It was such a relief that the rasper coincided with the goal but I feared that waiting for another goal from Ireland was going to stretch the limit of possibilities.

Oh joy of joys not so. Ireland were playing like a team possessed and being cheered on by the enthusiastic drinkers. I found myself nonchalantly striding up and down letting rip at an Olympian pace.

Tomorrow I attend the Yoga class which may not offer the same degree of cover.

I will report.

Iain Mac Clean

Exercise Four: *Paring Back*

There's a wonderful website called www.flylady.net which I discovered some years ago. Flylady tells you all about how to get on top of clutter and get your house and your life back. When I first discovered flylady I laughed. Her ideas seemed a bit out there. One of her guiding principles, for example, is that you begin to declutter your house by polishing your kitchen sink.

I came to eat my words. I can testify that flylady knows her stuff. A polished kitchen sink does lift your spirits! She also strongly believes in flinging stuff every day from your house; going around with a big plastic bag and dumping all the stuff you don't need. Now is there anything more therapeutic than doing just that?

The experience of illness can stop you in your tracks, make you wonder about why you spent all that time doing all that unnecessary stuff with your life. Often people emerge from a brush with a serious illness with a new sense of purpose about where they will focus their energies and what they will need to ditch from their lives. They find it much easier to separate the really important things from the rubbish.

James Pennebaker's wife, Ruth Pennebaker, the writer, in a joint address with her husband to the Breast Cancer Resource Centre, spoke about how, in the weeks following her diagnosis, this had affected her own life:

> It was just as if, with the diagnosis, I exchanged all these small fears for one enormous terror of dying and leaving my family. And it was

absolutely terrible but at the same time it freed me in a certain way. I finally had one great fear that was worthy of having. Some days I felt exhilarated. I felt that this strong wind had come in and had swept away everything that was not important in my life and only left things that were significant. I had a sense of clarity I'd never had in my life.

So what is it that you would pare back from your life?

Write a list of all the stuff/routines/jobs/people that are cluttering your life. Now write about your new pared-back version of your life. What is it like? What does your favourite room look like? Your office? How do you spend each day?

Exercise Five: *Illness and Metaphor*

Metaphor has been mentioned many times in this book but here it is again. Sometimes in dealing with painful subject matter, metaphor can be really useful as the following poem, as well as the introduction by the writer, shows:

> The night following my first surgery for breast cancer, I had a nightmare about a white lion. Frightened, I also sensed that the lion was inexplicably linked to me through a symbiotic relationship which was not always negative. When I awoke, my first thought was that he was my cancer. I composed this poem in my head that morning, as I lay in my hospital bed. Later, another thought was that 'he' might have been my surgeon (blonde female) who, by necessity, had to cut my body apart in order to 'save' me.

℘ *The White Lion*

The white lion
Bounds
Into my small garden
Ambles

Into the corner.
I am standing
In the centre.

Four walls and a roof
Slam
Into position
Clash of steel
Though these walls are
Thin
And
Tin,
My house.
Dark.
I am standing
In the centre
Turning
Looking
Eyeing.

His coat is
Golden
Labrador-like
In the light
Outside.
He is young
Healthy
Curious
Staring
Eyeing.
His threat
Unspoken
Bravado
But there.
He moves

Mere
Steps
Slight turn of his head
Firm
Stare
While I flee
Up
Steps
A path
Out Of my garden.
He can follow.

Marion Cox

So, in your own case, if this illness was an animal, what kind of animal
would it be?
Would it be a slithery snake? A charging rhino? An annoying, screeching
monkey?
Now write from the point of view of the animal you have chosen.

And Finally... while a diagnosis of a serious illness can feel like
everything has changed utterly, it isn't always the case. Reynolds Price, a
well-known American writer, described in his book, *A Whole New Life: An
Illness and a Healing*, how he survived a deeply traumatic diagnosis of spinal
cord cancer and came to terms with paralysis. Much like Stephen King,
whose experience of beginning to write again after a serious accident was
described in Chapter One, Reynolds Price also got on with the things he
knew had served him well. He does not make little of the profound impact
of his diagnosis and everything that happened to him. But right through
his illness over many years, he continued to write poems, kept a journal or,
if he couldn't write much, made entries in a calendar he kept. His book, *A
Whole New Life*, is a searing account of his harrowing experiences but in the
middle of it there are triumphs. His novel, *Kate Vaiden*, written during his

illness, won the National Book Critics Circle Award. He concludes his account of his experiences with the following: 'I write six days a week, long days that often run till bedtime; and the books are different from what came before in more ways than age. I sleep long nights with few hard dreams, and now I've outlived both my parents. Even my handwriting looks very little like the script of the man I was in June of '84. Cranky as it is, it's taller, more legible, with more air and stride. It comes down the arm of a grateful man.'

The final section of this book ends with a lot of suggestions of ways you can continue your writing; resources you might find useful.

SECTION THREE

Where To Go From Here

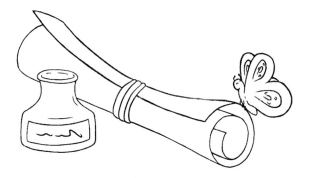

16

Resources

While there is a comprehensive list of all references at the end of the book, in this chapter I have compiled a list of resources which you may find helpful. You will find plenty more ideas, especially in the Gillie Bolton books which tend to focus on the practice of therapeutic writing with a lot of examples and methods.

Great Books
For people looking for more ideas on how to use writing as a way of exploring their own life or for ideas for their creative writing in poetry and fiction, the following is a list of books which you might find helpful to dip into for further ideas.

- Bolton, G.(1999) *The Therapeutic Potential of Creative Writing: Writing Myself*, Jessica Kingsley Publishers.

- Bolton, G. (2011) *Write Yourself: Creative Writing and Personal Development*, Jessica Kingsley Publishers.
  Like many of Gillie Bolton's books this very accessible book is useful for both practitioners who would like to know more about how to use this kind of writing and for the person who is writing for themselves.

- Bolton, G., Field, V. and Thompson, K. (eds) (2011) *Writing Routes: A Resource Handbook of Therapeutic Writing*, Jessica Kingsley Publishers.

This is a useful book for both therapists and, practitioners and beginning writers. It provides a lot of ideas for writing based on people's own experiences of trying them out.

- Davey, Julie (2007) *Writing for Wellness*, Idyll Arbor.
  This book describes the work of Julie Davey, a College Writing Professor, cancer survivor and facilitator of an ongoing group at City of Hope cancer centre in California. It's very accessible and gives a lot of ideas of practical exercises to try and also provides lots of extracts from the writing of participants.

- Evans, J. F. (ed.) (2010) *Wellness and Writing Connections: Writing for better physical, mental and spiritual health*, Idyll Arbor.
  This book pulls together a whole lot of practice-based papers from a recent conference on writing and wellbeing.

- Goldberg, N. (1986) *Writing Down the Bones*, Shambala.
  An oldie but a goodie. Natalie Goldberg provides a real sense of how writing can be done on a day-to-day basis based on her personal experience. She also places such writing firmly into a schema that embraces writing as meditation.

For Fiction Writers

There are vast arrays of books on how to write and how to edit. I am only going to mention two, both of which have already been cited in this book.

- King, Stephen (2000) *On Writing*, Hodder and Stoughton.
  This is a stalwart reference on most writing courses. It feels like Stephen King is right there in the room with you, his voice is so distinctive and his account of how he got back to writing after a serious accident is riveting.

- Brande, Dorothea (1934) *Becoming a Writer*, J. P. Tarcher.
  It's not often that you come across a book as good as this on the process of how to become a writer, how to see yourself as a writer, how to become a disciplined writer. What can I say? It's brilliant.

For Those Using Therapeutic Writing as a Way of Working with Clients or as a Way of Reflecting on their Own Work:

- Bolton, G. (2010) *Reflective Practice: Writing and Professional Development* (3rd Edition), Sage.
  This is particularly useful for those using writing as a way of reflecting on their own work.

- Bolton, G., Howlett, S., Lago, C., Wright, J. K. (eds) (2004) *Writing Cures: An Introductory Handbook of writing in counselling and therapy*, Routledge.

- Bolton, G., Field, V. and Thomson, K. (eds) (2006) *Writing Works: A resource Handbook for Therapeutic Writing Workshops and Activities*, Jessica Kinsgley Publishers.

- Frank, A. W. (1997) *The Wounded Storyteller: Body, Illness and Ethics*, The University of Chicago Press.

- Lepore, S. J. and Smyth, J. M. (eds) (2002) *The Writing Cure: How expressive writing promotes health and emotional well-being*, American Psychological Association.
  The focus of this book is on research in the field of writing and wellbeing.

- Moon, Jennifer, A. (2006) *Learning Journals: A Handbook for Reflective Practice and Professional Development*, Routledge.

- Pennebaker, J. (1990) *Opening up: the healing power of expressing emotions*, Guildford Press.

- Waters, T. (2004) *Therapeutic Storywriting: A Practical Guide to Developing Emotional Literacy in Primary Schools*, David Fulton Publishers.

Useful Websites

- *www.patriciamcadoo.ie*

My own website is a useful link, especially if you would like some feedback on any of your writing. I work online with anyone who wishes to avail of this. I also write a regular blog on Writing for Wellbeing.

- *www.gilliebolton.com*

What can I say about Gillie? She has been my mentor in all of the work I do. Her books (see under books!) are pure magic to read, everyone of which is a well-thumbed trove of ideas and exercises. She is a joy to work with and more than anyone else has fired me up with a love of this work. Her website gives a real flavour of how Gillie works and how she writes.

- *www.jkp.com*

A really useful site with good resources.

- *www.oneyearofwritingandhealing.com*

This website is a real gem giving lots of writing ideas for a whole year. I've used many of these in groups and they never fail to ignite good writing.

- *www.writingandhealing.org*

A more up-to-date version from the same author. But both of the websites here are just crammed full of ideas for writing from a great practitioner.

- *www.linkedin.com*

The Wellness and Writing subgroup on Linkedin provides a lot of information on what other people are doing. Good for people who are working in the field.

- *www.lapidus.org.uk*

A UK based organisation for anyone with an interest in writing and wellbeing. It has a membership list, regional groups and provides useful information about training events and conferences.

- *www.stumbleupon.com*

When you join up, you can register your interest in any writing and from time to time the people at StumbleUpon (there are people aren't there?) send out random web pages which you may or may not find interesting. I've cited one in this book and I do find some gems occasionally, though you can get a bit of repetition too.

- *www.livingwordsprogram.com*

Originally this programme was developed within the Psychology department at Wolford College, South Carolina as a writing programme for people with dementia and their carers. The programme is now used widely in the US with older people in groups. The website is full of useful information.

⚬✌   *www.ted.com*

I'm very fond of dipping into this website which features talks (usually eighteen minutes long) from leading experts in the field or people who are passionate about getting one big idea out to other people. The talks are themed and also rated.

⚬✌   *www.therapeuticstorywriting.com*

This website is very useful for those using writing with children in school settings (educational psychologists and teachers).

⚬✌   *www.storycubes.com*

I have used these cubes with adults and children as a way of sparking the imagination. They work very well and have also been used in Speech and Language Therapy. Some examples of the kind of stories children generate using them are on the website.

Concluding Words

I hope that you've enjoyed trying out some of the exercises in this book. Most of all I hope that you have found in these pages a sense of what Writing for Wellbeing is all about, how much fun it can be and how useful it can be to take up your pen and let off steam if something has upset you or puzzled you or made you laugh out loud. Maybe by now you have a record of such moments where your writing helped you to figure something out or to savour a great moment you might otherwise have forgotten all about.

When I had my first child, I kept a diary of the first year or so of his life, of our life together. I had given up work and was at home with him every day. It wasn't a 'when he cut his first tooth' sort of diary. I didn't focus on the milestones. Instead I wrote to try to capture something of what life was like, this whole new world of motherhood.

In there somewhere is a record of a glorious, crisp sunny morning when we went out to the harbour in Howth. After a stroll among the fish stands, we ended up in a cafe on the waterfront. I got my coffee. Bob Dylan played on the stereo. There were no other customers. The strong morning sunlight bathed us in warmth. I held him in my arms, gazing out to a perfectly still sea and we danced to the sound of 'Lay, lady, lay'.

There have been times in my life when writing has been of huge significance to me and other times when my notebook has gathered dust, ignored and unwanted. You may find the same thing: that there are days when you reach for this book for a writing idea and other times when you don't give writing a second thought.

What I know for certain is that writing has always been something to which I return. My notebook waits, like a faithful old dog, knowing that I will come back to it and I always do. There were many 'tear your hair out' moments in that first year as a mother. I often felt lonely and confused about why I had chosen to give up work and stay at home. Writing about that morning in the cafe crystallised something for me at that time – made me sure-footed, made me look at everything in a clear-eyed way. This was why I had done it, why I had walked away from my job, for moments like that. I am eternally grateful to my writing self that this hour, out of all the thousands of forgotten hours in that year, this one hour is recorded in my notebook.

Writing can help us to learn to be compassionate with ourselves. We can become the best version of ourselves through writing. The great thing is the journey continues. You buy another notebook and you start again!

References

Adcock, Fleur (2000), *Poems: 1960–2000*, Bloodaxe Books. The poem 'For Heidi with Blue Hair' was reprinted with kind permission from Bloodaxe Books.

Adams, Kathleen (1990), *Journal to the Self: Twenty-Two Paths to Personal Growth – Open the Door to Self-Understanding by Writing, Reading, and Creating a Journal of Your Life*, Grand Central Publishing.

Bettleheim, Bruno (1976/Reprinted 1991), *The Uses of Enchantment: The Meaning and Importance of Fairy Tales*, Penguin.

Bolton, Gillie, Field, Victoria, Thompson, Kate (eds) (2006), *Writing Works: A Resource Handbook for Therapeutic Writing Workshops and Activities*, Jessica Kingsley Publishers. The poem 'Take Care' by Gillie Bolton was reprinted with kind permission of Jessica Kinsgley Publishers.

Bolton, Gillie, Field, Victoria, Thompson, Kate (eds) (2011), *Writing Routes: A Resource Handbook of Therapeutic Writing*, Jessica Kingsley Publishers.

Bolton, Gillie (2011), *Write Yourself: Creative Writing and Personal Development*, Jessica Kingsley Publishers.

Brande, Dorothea (1934), *Becoming a Writer*, Harcourt, Brace and Company.

Buttimer, Angela (2010), 'Writing for Recovery: Working with Cancer Patients, Survivors and their Loved Ones', in Evans, John Frank (ed) *Wellness and Writing Connections: Writing for Better Physical, Mental and Spiritual Health*, Idyll Arbor, Inc.

Cummings, E. E. (1991), *Complete Poems, 1904–1962*, Liveright Publishing Corporation.

Dauby, Jean-Dominique (1997), *The Diving Bell and the Butterfly*, Harper Perennial.

Doyle, Roddy (2012), *Bullfighting*, Vintage.

Dr. Seuss (1990), *Oh, the Places You'll Go!*, Harper Collins.

Duke, M.P., Lazarus, A., & Fivush, R. (2008), *Knowledge of Family History as a Clinically Useful Index of Psychological Well-Being and Prognosis: A Brief Report*, Psychotherapy Theory, Research, Practice, Training, 45, 268–272.

Eliot, T. S. (2002) (new edition), *The Waste Land and Other Poems*, Faber and Faber.

Fainlight, Ruth (1983), *Fifteen to Infinity*, Hutchinson.

Feiler, Bruce, 'The Stories That Bind Us', *New York Times*, 15 March 2013.

Frank, Arthur W. (1995), *The Wounded Story Teller: Body, Illness and Ethics*, University of Chicago Press.

Geary, James (2012), *I Is an Other: The Secret Life of Metaphor and How it Shapes the Way We See the World*, Harper Collins.

Goldberg, Natalie (1986), *Writing Down the Bones: Freeing the Writer Within*, Shambala.

Goldberg, Natalie (2000), *Thunder and Lightning: Cracking Open the Writer's Craft*, Bantam Books.

Heaney, Seamus (1969; repr. 1991), *Death of a Naturalist*, Faber and Faber.

Heller, Joseph (2011), *Catch-22*, 50th anniversary reissue, Vintage Classics.

Karr, Mary (2010), *Lit: A Memoir*, Fourth Estate.

Kavanagh, Patrick (1964), *Collected Poems*, Martin, Brian and O'Keefe.

King, Stephen (2000), *On Writing: A Memoir of the Craft*, Hodder and Stoughton.

Lakoff, George and Johnson, Mark (1980), *Metaphors We Live By*, University of Chicago Press.

Lepore, Stephen, J. and Smyth, Joshua M. (eds) (2002), *The Writing Cure: How Expressive Writing Promotes Health and Emotional Well-Being*, American Psychological Association.

Lux, Thomas, 'The Voice You Hear When You Read Silently', published in *The New Yorker*, July, 1997.

Mc Gough, Roger (1981), *Strictly Private: An Anthology of Poetry*, Kestrel Books.

Martel, Yann (2001), *The Life of Pi*, 2001, Alfred A. Knopf.

Milne, A. A. and Shepherd, E. H. (1998), *A World of Winnie-the-Pooh: A Collection of Stories, Verses and Hums About the Bear of Very Little Brain*, Egmont Books.

Munro, H. H. (1993), *The Collected Short Stories of Saki*, Wordsworth Classics.

O' Brien, Tim (2009), *The Things They Carried*, Mariner Books.

O' Callaghan, Julie (2008), *Tell Me This is Normal: New and Selected Poems*, Bloodaxe Books.

Pennebaker, J. W. (1990), *Opening Up: The Healing Power of Expressing Emotions*, The Guildford Press.

Pennebaker, J. W. (1997), Writing About Emotional Experiences As A Therapeutic Process, *Psychological Science*, Vol. 8, No. 3.

Pennebaker, J. W. and Stone, L. D. (2003), 'Words of Wisdom: Language Use Over the Life Span', *Journal of Personality and Social Psychology*, 85, 291–301.

Pennebaker, J. W. and Chung, C. K. (2011), 'Expressive Writing: Connections to Physical and Mental Health', in H. S. Friedman (ed.), *Oxford Handbook of Health Psychology*, Oxford University Press.

Price, Reynolds (2003), *A Whole New Life: An Illness and a Healing*, Scribner.

Remen, Rachel (2000), *My Grandfather's Blessings: Stories of Strength, Refuge and Belonging*, Riverhead Books.

Roberts, Michèle (2008), *Paper Houses: A Memoir of the 1970s and beyond*, Virago Press.

Scott Fitzgerald, F. (1926), *The Great Gatsby*, Penguin Modern Classics (2000).

Shaughnessy, Lorna (2011), *Witness Trees*, Salmon Poetry. This poem was reprinted with kind permission from Salmon Poetry.

Smith, Dodie (1949, new edition 2004), *I Capture the Castle*, Vintage Classics.

Stein, Amelia (2011), *The Palm House*, Lilliput Press.

Whittle, Andrea and Mueller, Frank (2011), 'Bankers in the Dock: Moral Storytelling in Action', *Human Relations*, 65 (1).

Williams, Jonathan (1965), *Stoner*, New York Review Book.

Williams, Nick (1999), *The Work We Were Born To Do: Find the Work You Love, Love the Work You Do*, Element Books.

Wittgenstein, L., (1998), *Culture and Value*, ed. by Henrik von Wright, Wiley-Blackwell.

Yeats, William Butler (2008), 'Never Give All the Heart' originally printed in the collection *In the Seven Woods* (1904), Wordsworth Editions.